DR. FANATOMY

Poetry Prompts Book for Teens

Creative Writing Prompts to Boost Confidence, Self-Expression, and Emotional Clarity for Teen Girls and Boy

★ INSTA GUIDE
★ TRACK YOUR POEMS
★ MIND MAPS

copyright@ dr. fanatomy 2025

All rights reserved. No part of this publication may be reproduced, distributed, or transmitted in any form or by any means, including photocopying, recording, or other electronic or mechanical methods, without the prior written permission of the publisher, except in the case of brief quotations embodied in critical reviews and certain other noncommercial uses permitted by copyright law.

This book is a work of non-fiction, and any resemblance to actual persons, living or dead, or actual events is purely coincidental.

The information and techniques described in this book are intended for educational and informational purposes only. The author and publisher shall not be held liable for any injury, damage, or loss arising from using or misusing the information presented in this book.

While every effort has been made to ensure the accuracy of the information contained within this book, the author and publisher make no warranties or representations express or implied, about the completeness, accuracy, reliability, suitability, or availability with respect to the contents of this book for any purpose. The use of any information provided in this book is at the reader's own risk.

TABLE OF CONTENTS

INTRODUCTION: YOUR JOURNEY INTO POETRY STARTS HERE
(Pg:3-7)

- Hey there, awesome teen!
- Why Poetry Is Your Creative Superpower
- How to Use This Journal
- Setting Up Your Vibe: Create a Writing Space That Inspires
- Mind Map: Your Perfect Writing Space
- Visual Tool: Poetry Starter Table

CHAPTER 1: DISCOVER YOUR VOICE WITH CREATIVE WRITING PROMPTS
(Pg: 8-19)

- Hey there, creative soul!
- Why Your Voice Matters in Poetry and Life
- Table: Why Your Voice Is Awesome
- Table: What Shapes Your Story
- Breaking Writing Fears
- Prompt Practice: First Feelings
- Visual Tool: Voice Finder Mind Map
- Table: Quick Reference – Finding and Using Your Poetic Voice
- Activity Zone and Answers
- Quick Reference – Finding and Using Your Poetic Voice

CHAPTER 2: CONQUERING THE BLANK PAGE
(Pg: 20-28)

- Hey, Awesome Teen Poet!
- Table: Why Conquering the Blank Page Rocks
- What's Holding You Back?
- Table: Common Writing Blocks and Quick Fixes
- Emotions to Ink
- Table: Emotions to Imagery

TABLE OF CONTENTS

- Prompt Practice: Kickoff Lines
- Table: Kickoff Line Prompts
- Visual Tool: Blank Page Buster Table
- Blank Page Buster Mind Map
- Activity Zone and Answers

CHAPTER 3: EMOTIONAL CLARITY THROUGH POETRY
(Pg: 29-39)

- Hey, Amazing Teen Poet!
- Poetry as Your Emotional Outlet
- Writing Through Big Feels
- Let Go of Perfection
- Table: Beat Perfectionism
- Prompt Practice: Mood Follow Me
- Visual Tool: Emotion Wheel
- Visual Tool: Emotional Clarity Mind Map
- Activity Zone and Answers

CHAPTER 4: WHO YOU ARE: IDENTITY IN VERSE
(Pg:40-52)

- Learning Objectives
- Using Poetry to Explore Your Identity
- Table: Why Identity Poetry Shines
- Table: Defining Your Identity
- Poetry as Your Mirror
- Prompt Practice: Your Story in Verse
- 5 Identity Prompts
- Visual Tool: Identity Map
- Your Turn: Reflective Journal Page
- Activity Zone and Answers

TABLE OF CONTENTS

CHAPTER 5: CRAFTING AESTHETIC VIBES IN POETRY

(Pg: 53-65)

- Learning Objectives
- Introduction: Making Poems Pop with Style and Mood
- Table: Why Aesthetic Poetry Slays
- Setting the Tone
- Imagery That Shines
- Prompt Practice: Your Story in Verse
- Visual Tool: Aesthetic Mood Board Table
- Your Turn: Reflective Journal Page
- Visual Tool: Aesthetic Vibe Mind Map
- Activity Zone and Answers

CHAPTER 6: POEMS FOR FRIENDS, FAMILY, AND FEELS

(Pg:66-79)

- Learning Objectives
- Introduction: Poetry for the People You Love
- Table: Why Relationship Poetry Slays
- Celebrating Connections
- Quick Craft Tip
- Healing Through Verse
- Prompt Practice: Letter Poems
- Table: Letter Poem Prompts
- Visual Tool: Relationship Web
- Your Turn: Fill This Out!
- Visual Tool: Relationship Connection Mind Map
- Activity Zone and Answers

TABLE OF CONTENTS

CHAPTER 7: HOLIDAY VIBES: SEASONAL POETRY PROMPTS
(Pg: 80 -93)

- Capturing Holiday Magic in Verse
- Table: Why Holiday Poetry Slays
- Christmas and Winter Wonders
- Table: Christmas and Winter Wonders
- Thanksgiving and Gratitude
- Prompt Practice: Holiday Glow
- Visual Tool: Holiday Prompt Planner
- Your Turn: Reflective Journal Page
- Visual Tool: Holiday Connection Mind Map
- Activity Zone and Answers

CHAPTER 8: CRAFT, SHARE, AND COLLECT YOUR POETRY
(Pg: 94-107)

- Learning Objectives
- Why Crafting, Sharing, and Collecting Poetry Is Your Superpower
- Poetry Styles That Pop
- Building Your Poetry Legacy
- Prompt Practice: Style, Share, Collect
- Example Exercise
- Visual Tool: Poetry Creation Mind Map
- Your Turn: Reflective Journal Page
- Peer Review Quick Guide
- Activity Zone and Answers

CHAPTER 9 : POETRY LEGACY LAB: YOUR STORY IN VERSE
(Pg: 108 -116)

- Learning Objectives
- Prompt Practice: 10 Poem Challenge
- Visual Tool: Poetry Legacy Mind Map
- Your Turn: Reflective Journal Page

TABLE OF CONTENTS

CONCLUSION & BONUS (Pg: 117-122)

APPENDIX (Pg:123-126)

- Appendix -A : Poetry Power Words
- Appendix -B : Poetry Starters
- Appendix - C : How to Approach Poetry
- Appendix - d : Common Grammar Fixes for Poetry

Introduction: Your Journey Into Poetry Starts Here

Your Journey Into Poetry Starts Here

📣 **Hey there, awesome teen!**

Welcome to Poetry Journal for Teens: Creative Writing Prompts to Boost Confidence, Self-Expression, and Emotional Clarity. Whether you're a dreamer, a deep thinker, a quiet observer, or just trying to figure out life, this journal is your creative sidekick.

Poetry is like a superpower—it helps you express who you are, sort through emotions, and create something that's 100% YOU. It doesn't matter if you're new to writing or already dropping poems on Instagram—this journal is for you. Let's dive into what makes poetry your secret weapon—and how this journal will guide you one page at a time.

💥 Why Poetry Is Your Creative Superpower

"Poetry is when an emotion has found its thought and the thought has found words." —Robert Frost

You might think poetry is just for school assignments or old-timey writers, but it's way more powerful (and fun!) than that. Poetry is:

🔑 Benefit	💬 Why It Matters
Boosts Confidence	Every line you write is a reminder that your voice matters. And it totally does. Creative writing helps teens build self-esteem and speak up.
A Safe Space to Be Real	You can write about love, fear, dreams, or random thoughts—without anyone judging you.
A Way to Process Big Emotions	From family drama to school stress, poetry helps you make sense of the chaos. (Bonus: it supports Social-Emotional Learning or SEL in U.S. school curriculums!)
A Brain Booster	Poetry sharpens your thinking and writing skills—hello, better essays, SAT scores, and college apps!

📌 Example: Poem by Mia, age 15 (Chicago)

Storm clouds in my chest,
Words spill like rain.
I write, and suddenly,
I'm not alone.

Mia wrote this after a rough week. Just four lines—and she felt lighter. That's the power of poetry!

✍️ How to Use This Journal

This isn't a workbook. It's your creative playground. Here's how to make it work for you:

- **Start with Prompts**: Prompts are mini-invitations to write. Example: "Write a poem about a moment you felt unstoppable."
- **Try New Styles**: From free verse (no rules!) to haikus (5-7-5) and blackout poetry, you'll get to experiment with forms.
- **Use the Creative Tools**: This journal includes tables, charts, and mind maps to spark ideas. (Like the Poetry Starter Table below!)
- **Write for Yourself**: No grades. No pressure. Just you, your thoughts, and the page.
- **Create a Daily Habit**: Even 5–10 minutes a day makes a difference. Use your fave playlist and vibe out while you write.

🧠 Pro Tip for Parents, Teachers, and Homeschoolers:

This journal:
- Aligns with Common Core writing standards
- Supports Social-Emotional Learning (SEL)
- Helps teens build a writing portfolio
- It's a perfect Q4 holiday or birthday gift

Whether you're using this in class, at home, or as part of a writing club, this is more than a journal; it's a confidence-building toolkit for teens.

✨ Setting Up Your Vibe: Create a Writing Space That Inspires

Your writing space should feel like your zone—a place where ideas flow and distractions disappear. Here's a mind map to help you design your perfect poetry corner:

🧭 Mind Map: Your Perfect Writing Space

```
[Your Writing Space]
├── Location
│   ├── Quiet (Bedroom, Library)
│   ├── Nature (Park, Backyard)
│   └── Public (Café, School)
├── Vibes
│   ├── Lighting (Fairy Lights, Lamp)
│   ├── Decor (Vision Board, Posters)
│   └── Comfort (Beanbag, Blanket)
├── Tools
│   ├── Journal or Laptop
│   ├── Colorful Pens
│   └── Headphones
└── Mood
    ├── Playlist (Lo-fi, Taylor Swift, Indie Rock)
    ├── Snacks (Fruit, Chips)
    └── Drinks (Tea, Smoothie)
```

Example: Jake, 16, transformed his desk into a poetry cave, complete with a lava lamp, a notebook adorned with skateboarding stickers, and a chill indie playlist. He says it's like "hanging out with my thoughts."

🚀 Ready to Write?

This journal is your space to shine—whether you're:

- Writing for fun
- Exploring your identity
- Using it in class
- Building a scholarship-ready portfolio

⚡ Visual Tool: Poetry Starter Table

Stuck? This table gives you quick inspiration. Mix and match emotions, starter words, and imagery to spark a poem.

😀 Emotion	🔤 Starter Words	🖼️ Imagery Ideas
Joy	sparkle, soar, glow	sunflowers, fireworks, warm breeze
Anger	burn, shatter, scream	thunder, cracked glass, red flames
Sadness	fade, drift, ache	rainy window, wilted flower, gray sky
Hope	rise, bloom, shine	sunrise, open road, new leaves
Fear	tremble, shadow, freeze	dark woods, flickering light, tight hallway

Chapter 1: Discover Your Voice with Creative Writing Prompts

Discover Your Voice with Creative Writing Prompts

Hey there, creative soul!

Welcome to your poetry journey—this chapter is your launchpad. Whether you're brand new to poetry or already scribbling in notebooks, here's the truth: your voice matters. It's how you express your feelings, ideas, dreams, and identity. It's like your favorite playlist—totally you and worth sharing.

- We're going to explore:
- What makes your voice unique
- Why it's powerful to share your story
- How to beat writing fears
- Fun prompts and poems from real teens
- 4 activities with questions to help sharpen your skills
- Let's get started—your story deserves to be heard.

💬 Why Your Voice Matters in Poetry and Life

Because no one else sees the world exactly the way you do.

Your background, hobbies, beliefs, and emotions shape your creative voice. Plus, writing poetry builds real-world skills. According to the National Council of Teachers of English (NCTE), creative writing boosts self-esteem, emotional intelligence, and school success—it's even linked to better performance on standardized tests like the SAT and ACT.

✨ *Think about poets like Amanda Gorman, who inspired a nation, or Rupi Kaur, who turned emotion into bestselling books. They started by writing from the heart—just like you can.*

Table: Why Your Voice Is Awesome

Benefit	How It Helps	Example
Confidence	You feel proud of what you create	A poem about your love for baking
Emotional Clarity	You understand and name your feelings	A poem about being nervous before a test
School Success	You write stronger essays and stories	Using vivid imagery in a class assignment
Real Connection	You express yourself in ways others feel	Sharing a poem on Instagram #YoungWriters

📝 Example Poem by Jaden, 15, Atlanta

City lights pulse like my dreams,
Concrete jungle, I'm alive.
My words carve a path through the noise.

Jaden said this poem made him feel "seen." That's what your voice can do—make you feel powerful and heard.

✨ Owning Your Story

Your story is the core of your voice. The highs (winning a match), the lows (losing a friend), and the quirks (like your obsession with stickers or sneakers)—they all shape your poetry.

Table: What Shapes Your Story

Category	Questions to Ask	Poem Idea
Passions	What do I love doing?	A poem about dancing at midnight
Challenges	What have I faced?	A poem about changing schools
Culture	What traditions matter to me?	A poem about Eid, Diwali, or Thanksgiving
Quirks	What makes me unique?	A poem about your lucky socks

Example Poem by Aisha, 16, Chicago

Henna swirls tell my story,
Spices dance in Mama's pot.
My roots bloom in every line.

📌 Try this:

List three things that define you. Choose one and turn it into the first line of a poem. This helps build narrative writing skills and supports SEL reflection.

🚫 Breaking Writing Fears

Let's be real—writing can feel scary. You might wonder, "What if it's bad?" or "What if people laugh?" Don't worry. Even famous poets started with crumpled pages.

Table: Busting Common Writing Fears

Fear	Truth	Action Step
"I'm not creative."	Creativity grows with practice.	Write nonstop for 5 minutes. No edits!
"I'll be judged."	Your journal = your safe space.	Share only when you feel ready.
"I don't know how."	Prompts make it easy to start.	Use a starter line or the mind map below.
"It won't be good."	First drafts are never perfect.	Write a silly poem to break the pressure.

Example Poem by Mia, 14, Texas

Rewrite each formal line as if texting a friend (≤12 words, emojis welcome).

My backpack's stuffed, a total mess,
Books and dreams in a tangle, I guess

🧠 Prompt Practice: First Feelings

Use these writing prompts to express how you feel. These are short, focused, and perfect for building confidence. Set a 10-minute timer and write freely.

Table 5: First-Feeling Prompts

Prompt #	Title	Starter Line	Sample Line
1	Proud Moment	"I stood tall when…"	I stood tall when I spoke up in class.
2	Emotion as Color	"My [emotion] is a shade of…"	My joy is a shade of sunrise orange.
3	Superpower Dream	"If I could [superpower], I'd…"	If I could fly, I'd explore the clouds.
4	Nature Vibes	"In this place, I…"	In this park, I feel the trees breathing.
5	Future Dream	"One day, I'll…"	One day, I'll perform on a Broadway stage.

📝 Example Poem (Prompt 3: Superpower)

If I could time-travel, I'd leap ahead,
See my future, no fear, no dread.
Back to now, I'd write my way,
Every word a step to that day.

🧭 Visual Tool: Voice Finder Mind Map

Here's a visual tool to brainstorm your voice. Start with "Your Voice" in the center and build out.

[Your Voice]
├── Emotions → joy, fear, anger, calm
├── Experiences → big events, funny moments
├── Dreams → goals, travel, inventions
└── Values → fairness, kindness, courage

📝 Example Poem Using Mind Map

Excitement sparks like a concert's roar,
My first show, music, opened the door.
One day, I'll strum my wild tune,
Creativity's fire, my heart's full moon.

Use this map when you're stuck—it works!

📚 Table: Quick Reference – Finding and Using Your Poetic Voice

Element	What It Means	How It Shows in Your Poetry	Why It Matters
Voice	Your unique style, experiences, and tone	Honest, real lines that sound like you	Builds confidence and makes your writing stand out
Tone	The feeling or vibe of your poem	Joyful, sad, hopeful, angry, etc.	Helps readers connect emotionally with your writing
Imagery	Descriptive language that paints a picture	"The wind whispered secrets in the trees"	Makes poems more vivid and memorable
Poetic Devices	Tools like similes, metaphors, rhyme, alliteration	"My thoughts are tangled like headphones in my pocket"	Adds rhythm, beauty, and meaning to your writing
Personal Connection	Drawing from your real-life thoughts, feelings, and dreams	Writing about your culture, hobbies, fears, or goals	Builds emotional clarity and self-awareness
Writing Confidence	Believing in your creative power	Taking writing risks, finishing drafts, sharing when ready	Helps you grow as a student, thinker, and communicator
Prompt Power	Using prompts to get started	"If I could fly…" or "One day, I'll…"	Gets your ideas flowing even when you're unsure what to write
Reflection	Looking back at what you wrote to learn from it	Reading your poems and noticing your voice and feelings in them	Encourages emotional growth and builds resilience
Growth Mindset	Knowing your writing will improve with time and practice	Revising poems, trying new styles, writing consistently	Helps you stay motivated and keep improving
Creative Freedom	Trusting yourself to write what feels true	Expressing anything—from silly socks to deep dreams	There are no wrong answers in poetry—it's your space to be free and real

🎯 ACTIVITY ZONE

ACTIVITY 1 – ANALYZING TONE IN A POEM

Poem by Kayla, 15, California:

The beach hums with a golden glow,
Waves whisper secrets only I know.
My heart dances with the tide's soft pull,
Free, alive, my soul feels full.

Questions:

1. What is the tone of Kayla's poem?
 a) Angry   b) Joyful   c) Sad   d) Confused

2. Which emotion is most prominent?
   1.a) Fear   b) Happiness   c) Frustration   d) Doubt

3. What imagery shows her feelings?
a) Dark clouds   b) Golden glow and waves   c) Broken glass   d) Flickering lights

4. True or False: The poem reflects Kayla's connection to nature.

5. Which line shows her sense of freedom?

a) "The beach hums with a golden glow"
b) "Waves whisper secrets only I know"
c) "Free, alive, my soul feels full"
d) "My heart dances with the tide's soft pull"

🎯 ACTIVITY ZONE

ACTIVITY 2 - IDENTIFYING VOICE ELEMENTS

Poem by Ethan, 16, Ohio:

My controller clicks, the screen's my stage,
Pixels battle, my heart's all rage.
One day, I'll code my own epic game,
My name in lights, my claim to fame.

Questions:

1. What's Ethan's passion?

 a) Cooking   b) Gaming   c) Reading   d) Traveling

2. What's his dream?
 a) Be a chef   b) Code a game   c) Write a book   d) Be an actor

3. True or False: Ethan uses tech imagery.

4. What emotion is present?
a) Calm   b) Sadness   c) Excitement   d) Fear

5. Which line shows ambition?
 a) "My controller clicks…"
 b) "Pixels battle…"
 c) "One day, I'll code…"
 d) "My name in lights…"

ACTIVITY 3 – SPOTTING POETIC DEVICES

Poem by Priya, 14, New Jersey:

My anger burns like a summer blaze,
Words sharp as thorns in a tangled maze.
I write to cool the fire in my chest,
Each line is a step toward finding rest.

Questions:

1) What device is "burns like a summer blaze"?
 a) Metaphor   b) Simile   c) Alliteration   d) Rhyme

2) What emotion dominates the poem?
a) Love   b) Anger   c) Hope   d) Joy

3) True or False: Every line rhymes.

4) What image shows anger?
a) Starry sky   b) Summer blaze   c) Calm ocean   d) Falling snow

5) What does writing do for her?
a) Confuses her   b) Makes her tired   c) Helps her feel calm   d) Makes her angrier

ACTIVITY 4 – UNDERSTANDING VALUES

Poem by Priya, 14, New Jersey:

My anger burns like a summer blaze,
Words sharp as thorns in a tangled maze.
I write to cool the fire in my chest,
Each line is a step toward finding rest.

Questions:

1) What value is shown?
 a) Kindness   b) Justice   c) Creativity   d) Loyalty

2) What image shows that value?
a) River   b) Oak tree   c) Star   d) Breeze

3) True or False: Liam is unsure of his beliefs.

4) What does he say about his voice?
a) It's loud   b) It may shake   c) It's perfect   d) It's silent

5) Which line shows fairness?

a) "Justice stands…"
b) "Strong and steady…"
c) "I speak for truth…"
d) "Fairness my guide…"

Final Words

This chapter helped you discover the power of your voice through poems, prompts, and practice. Keep your journal nearby—your next favorite poem is only one idea away.

Tip: This makes a perfect journal for school projects, creative writing electives, or a meaningful gift to encourage self-expression!

ANSWERS
ACTIVITY ZONE

ACTIVITY 1: ANALYZING TONE IN A POEM

Answers
1) b
2) b
3) b
4) True
5) c

ACTIVITY 2: IDENTIFYING VOICE ELEMENTS

Answers
1) b
2) b
3) True
4) c
5) c

ACTIVITY 3: SPOTTING POETIC DEVICES

Answers
1) b
2) b
3) False
4) b
5) c

ACTIVITY 4: UNDERSTANDING VALUES

Answers
1) b
2) b
3) False
4) b
5) d

Quick Reference – Finding and Using Your Poetic Voice

Element	What It Means	How It Shows in Your Poetry	Why It Matters
Voice	Your unique style, experiences, and tone	Honest, real lines that sound like you	Builds confidence and makes your writing stand out
Tone	The feeling or vibe of your poem	Joyful, sad, hopeful, angry, etc.	Helps readers connect emotionally with your writing
Imagery	Descriptive language that paints a picture	"The wind whispered secrets in the trees"	Makes poems more vivid and memorable
Poetic Devices	Tools like similes, metaphors, rhyme, alliteration	"My thoughts are tangled like headphones in my pocket"	Adds rhythm, beauty, and meaning to your writing
Personal Connection	Drawing from your real-life thoughts, feelings, and dreams	Writing about your culture, hobbies, fears, or goals	Builds emotional clarity and self-awareness
Writing Confidence	Believing in your creative power	Taking writing risks, finishing drafts, sharing when ready	Helps you grow as a student, thinker, and communicator
Prompt Power	Using prompts to get started	"If I could fly..." or "One day, I'll..."	Gets your ideas flowing even when you're unsure what to write
Reflection	Looking back at what you wrote to learn from it	Reading your poems and noticing your voice and feelings in them	Encourages emotional growth and builds resilience
Growth Mindset	Knowing your writing will improve with time and practice	Revising poems, trying new styles, writing consistently	Helps you stay motivated and keep improving
Creative Freedom	Trusting yourself to write what feels true	Expressing anything—from silly socks to deep dreams	There are no wrong answers in poetry—it's your space to be free and real

Chapter 2 : Conquering the Blank Page

CHAPTER 2 – CONQUERING THE BLANK PAGE

🌟 Hey, Awesome Teen Poet!

Staring at a blank page can feel like facing the final boss in a video game—overwhelming and unbeatable. But here's the truth: you already have what it takes to win. That blank space? It's not a wall—it's a launchpad.

In this chapter, you'll learn how to:
- Break through common writing blocks
- Transform emotions into expressive poetry
- Use vivid imagery to fuel your words
- Tap into smart, creative prompts
- Practice with powerful, fun activities that build confidence

You'll also find examples from real teens, reflection tables, and closed-ended questions perfect for classrooms, homeschool, or solo writing time.

✏️ Table: Why Conquering the Blank Page Rocks

Benefit	How It Helps	Example
Confidence	Makes you feel like a creative boss	Writing a poem about a tough day
Self-Expression	Lets you share your voice and story	A poem about your favorite hobby
Academic Success	Sharpens skills for essays, exams & ELA	Using vivid words in a book report
Emotional Clarity	Helps you process feelings in healthy ways	A poem about a friend fight

💬 "The blank page stares, but I stare back.
Pen in hand, I'm ready to attack."
—Zoe, 15, Oregon

Zoe said this poem helped her feel unstoppable. Now it's your turn.

✋ What's Holding You Back?

Writer's block is normal. Teens often get stuck because of:

- Overthinking
- Fear of "bad" writing
- Distractions
- Low motivation
-

Here's a table to help bust those blocks.

🚧 Table: Common Writing Blocks and Quick Fixes

Block	Why It Happens	Quick Fix
"I don't know where to start"	Too many or zero ideas	Write **one word** and build from it
"My writing's not good enough"	Fear of being judged	Freewrite for 5 minutes—**no editing**
"I'm too distracted"	Phone, noise, stress	**Set a timer**, find a quiet space
"I'm not inspired"	Feeling drained or flat	Use a **prompt** or listen to music

💬 *"Storm in my head, clouds collide,*
Pen scratches, and I'm along for the ride."

—Jamal, 16, Florida

Try this: Pick a block above, apply the fix, and write for 5 minutes.

🤍 Emotions to Ink

Poetry is emotion in motion. Whether you're hyped, hurt, or chill, your feelings fuel your art. The secret? Turn emotions into vivid images.

Poetry is emotion in motion. Whether you're hyped, hurt, or chill, your feelings fuel your art. The secret? Turn emotions into vivid images.

🎨 Table: Emotions to Imagery

Emotion	Image Ideas	Starter Words
Happiness	Sunlight, bubbles, balloons	glow, dance, rise
Anger	Fire, cracked glass, thunder	burn, crash, snap
Sadness	Rain, fog, shadows	drift, sink, fade
Excitement	Fireworks, racing cars	rush, blast, soar

💬 *"Rain taps my window, soft and slow,
My sadness drips, but words still flow."*
—Sophia, 14, Texas

Try this: Pick an emotion from the table, choose one image, and write a 4-line poem.

🚀 Prompt Practice: Kickoff Lines

Prompts = instant writing fuel. These five are perfect for teens and aligned with Common Core goals.

⚡ Table: Kickoff Line Prompts

#	Title	Prompt	Prompt
1	Victory Vibe	"I felt unstoppable when…"	I felt unstoppable when I crossed the line.
2	Emotion Snapshot	"This feeling looks like…"	This feeling looks like a neon spark.
3	Dream Destination	"If I could go anywhere, I'd…"	If I could go anywhere, I'd surf the stars.
4	Everyday Magic	"In my world, this shines…"	In my world, my playlist shines.
5	Future You	"In five years, I see…"	In five years, I see my art on walls.

💬 *"I felt unstoppable when I hit that note,*
Stage lights blazing, my voice afloat."

How to Use: Choose a prompt, set a 10-minute timer, and let your imagination run wild.

🔓 **Visual Tool: Blank Page Buster Table**
Your go-to guide for smashing blocks and starting poems.

🛠 **Table: Blank Page Buster**

Block	Solution	Starter Prompt
"I don't know where to start"	Write one word and build	"Thunder…"
"My writing's not good enough"	Write a "bad" poem on purpose	"My socks smell like…"
"I'm too distracted"	Write about the distraction	"My phone buzzes, but…"
"I'm not inspired"	Describe something in the room	"The lamp glows like…"
"I'm stuck on one idea"	Switch to a new emotion or image	"Joy feels like…"

💬 *"The lamp glows like a tiny moon,*
Casting dreams across my room."

—*Liam, 17, NY*

Visual Tool: Blank Page Buster Mind Map

This mind map helps you brainstorm ways to conquer the blank page. Start with "Conquer the Blank Page" in the center, then branch out to explore strategies, emotions, and inspirations to spark your writing.

```
[Conquer the Blank Page]
    ├── Strategies
    │     ├── Write one word
    │     ├── Use a prompt
    │     ├── Write a "bad" poem
    │     └── Describe what you see
    ├── Emotions
    │     ├── Happiness (e.g., sunlight)
    │     ├── Anger (e.g., fire)
    │     ├── Sadness (e.g., rain)
    │     └── Excitement (e.g., fireworks)
    ├── Inspirations
    │     ├── Music (e.g., favorite playlist)
    │     ├── Nature (e.g., park, sky)
    │     ├── Objects (e.g., phone, desk)
    │     └── Memories (e.g., a fun day)
    └── Goals
          ├── Fill one page
          ├── Write for 5 minutes
          ├── Try a new prompt
          └── Share with a friend
```

Example Poem Using Mind Map (Strategy: Write one word, Emotion: Excitement, Inspiration: Music, Goal: Fill one page):

Spark.
My playlist pumps, excitement's flame,
Beats fuel my pen, no pause, no shame.
The page fills fast, my heart's own game.

Use this mind map to plan your next poem. Pick one idea from each branch and write for 5–10 minutes. Homeschoolers, this is a great tool for brainstorming and creative planning.

ACTIVITY ZONE

ACTIVITY 1: ANALYZING A POEM'S START

Poem by Mia, 15 (California):

My phone buzzes, but I'm still here,
Words like sparks light up my fear.
The screen fades, my pen takes hold,
This page is mine, my story bold.

Questions:
1. Which writing block does Mia address?
2. What solution does she use?
3. True/False: The poem uses tech-related imagery.
4. What emotion is central?
5. Which line shows her taking control?

ACTIVITY 2 – IDENTIFY THE FRAGMENT

Poem by Ethan, 16 (Ohio):

Joy feels like a rocket's blaze,
Shooting high through summer days.
My pen races, words ignite,
The blank page burns with light.

Questions:
1. What emotion is shown?
2. What image matches that emotion?
3. True/False: The poem uses a simile.
4. Which prompt likely inspired Ethan?
5. What does this poem say about writing?

◎ ACTIVITY ZONE
ACTIVITY 3: SPOTTING THE SOLUTION

Poem by Aisha, 14 (Chicago):

Thunder rumbles in my mind,
One word sparks, and thoughts unwind.
The page fills fast, no time to wait,
My storm of words decides my fate.

Questions:
1. What block does Aisha face?
2. What's her fix?
3. True/False: Her first word was "thunder."
4. What's her imagery?
5. Which line shows momentum?

ACTIVITY 4: UNDERSTANDING IMAGERY

Poem by Liam, 17 (New York):

The lamp glows like a midnight star,
Guiding words from near to far.
My pen moves, the blank page sings,
Light and ink grow shining wings.

Questions:

1. What block is Liam tackling?
2. What solution did he use?
3. True/False: He uses a metaphor.
4. What's the central image?
5. Which line shows the page coming alive?

ANSWERS
ACTIVITY ZONE

ACTIVITY 1 – ANALYZING A POEM'S START

1. b) "I'm too distracted"
2. b) Wrote about the distraction
3. True
4. b) Fear
5. d) "This page is mine, my story bold"

ACTIVITY 2 – IDENTIFYING EMOTION IN POETRY

1. b) Joy
2. a) A rocket's blaze
3. True
4. b) "This feeling looks like…"
5. b) It's exciting and powerful

ACTIVITY 3 – SPOTTING THE SOLUTION

1. b) "I don't know where to start"
2. a) Write one word and build from it
3. True
4. b) A storm
5. c) "The page fills fast, no time to wait"

ACTIVITY 4 – UNDERSTANDING IMAGERY

1. c) "I'm not inspired"
2. b) Describe something he sees
3. False (It's a simile, not a metaphor)
4. a) A midnight star
5. c) "The blank page sings"

Chapter 3: Emotional Clarity Through Poetry

29

CHAPTER 3 – Emotional Clarity Through Poetry

🌀 Hey, Amazing Teen Poet!

Hey, incredible teen! Ready to turn your big, bold, messy feelings into poetry? This chapter is your safe space to explore emotions—whether you're buzzing with joy, tangled in stress, or just feeling meh. Poetry is like your best friend who listens without judging, helping you make sense of what's going on inside. We'll show you how to channel those feelings, ditch perfectionism, and write poems that feel like you. With tables, examples, prompts, an emotion wheel, activities, and a mind map, you'll be writing with emotional clarity in no time. Perfect for journaling, school, or sharing on Instagram, this chapter is your guide to unlocking your heart. Let's dive in!

📋 Poetry as Your Emotional Outlet

Being a teen means deep emotions—one moment you're thrilled about something new, the next you're overwhelmed. Poetry gives those emotions a voice. According to many research , writing about feelings supports emotional intelligence, stress management, and expression—key goals in U.S. SEL curricula aligned with Common Core standards.

Just like poets such as Rupi Kaur or Langston Hughes, your honest words can become powerful art. This chapter helps you tap into that power.

Benefit	How It Helps	Example
Emotional Clarity	Helps you name and process your feelings	A poem about anxiety before a test
Confidence	Validates your voice and experiences	Writing about happy memories
Descriptive Skills	Enhances expressive writing for essays	Using emotional language in class
Connection	Makes your feelings relatable to others	Sharing with peers under #TeenPoet

Example: Here's a poem by Riley, a 15-year-old from Michigan:

*My heart's a storm, all thunder and rain,
But words on this page ease the pain.
Each line's a step to a clearer sky.*

Riley said, "Writing this helped me feel calm for the first time in weeks." Let's make poetry your emotional outlet!

Writing Through Big Feels

SBig emotions—like joy, stress, or loneliness—can feel like a lot, but poetry is the perfect way to channel them. Name the feeling, give it an image, and let your words flow. Whether you're pumped about a win or wrestling with worry, writing helps you understand yourself better.

Table: Turning Emotions into Poems

Emotion	Image Ideas	Starter Words
Stress	Choppy seas, knot in rope	tense, churn, crack
Joy	Fireworks, sunrise	burst, glow, lift
Loneliness	Empty room, fading star	quiet, drifting, hollow
Hope	Blooming garden, sunrise	climb, shine, open

💬 *"Loneliness sits in an empty room,
Shadows stretch, a quiet gloom…"*
—Ethan, 16, Arizona

Try this: Pick one emotion and image from the table and write a 4-line poem.

Let Go of Perfection

Perfection can stop your poetry before it starts. You don't need rhyme. You don't need deep. You just need honesty. The most powerful poems grow from being real—even messy or silly.

✂ Table: Beat Perfectionism

Perfectionist Thought	Truth	Action Step
"It has to rhyme."	Free verse is effective too.	Write without rhyme.
"It's not deep enough."	Simple feelings are powerful.	Write one true line.
"It sounds silly."	Silly can be meaningful.	Write a goofy poem.
"It's not finished."	Rough drafts build your skill.	Stop after 5 minutes.

💬 *"My stress is a sock lost in the wash…"*
—Lila, 14, Ohio

Took Lila five minutes. Then she laughed—and paused the pressure. Try the same.

Prompt Practice: Mood Follow Me

Ready to write something real? Here are five emotion-driven prompts to help your heart translate into verse.

☀ Table: Mood Magic Prompts

Prompt #	Title	Starter Line	Example
1	Emotional Peak	"When I felt this, I…"	When I felt joy, I danced with stars.
2	Mood as Weather	"My mood is a…"	My mood is a thunderstorm—wild and bold.
3	Hidden Feeling	"Deep inside, I hide…"	Deep inside, I hide a quiet fear.
4	Emotional Place	"This place holds my…"	This place holds my calm, my soft breeze.
5	Future Mood	"Someday, I'll feel…"	Someday, I'll feel light as a kite.

Example Poem :

*Deep inside, I hide a quiet fear,
A shadow creeping, cold and near.
My words build a bridge to brighter days,
Fear fades in my poem's soft rays.*

How to Use: Pick one prompt, set a timer for 10 minutes, and write. If you're stuck, use the Emotion Wheel below. Teachers, these prompts are great for class assignments or portfolios. Parents, they're perfect for helping teens explore emotions.

🧠 Visual Tool: Emotion Wheel

his emotion wheel helps you pinpoint your feelings and turn them into poetry. Start with a core emotion in the center, then branch out to specific feelings to inspire your writing.

```
[Core Emotion]
    ├── Happy
    │   ├── Excited
    │   ├── Content
    │   └── Proud
    ├── Sad
    │   ├── Lonely
    │   ├── Hurt
    │   └── Disappointed
    ├── Angry
    │   ├── Frustrated
    │   ├── Annoyed
    │   └── Furious
    └── Afraid
        ├── Nervous
        ├── Anxious
        └── Scared
```

Example Poem Using Emotion Wheel (Core: Happy, Specific: Proud):

*Proud like a flag waving high,
My heart soars beneath the sky.
I wrote my truth, I stood up tall,
This page holds my victory call.*

Use the emotion wheel to pick a specific feeling and write a poem. Homeschoolers, this is a great tool for emotional awareness and writing practice.

Visual Tool: Emotional Clarity Mind Map

This mind map helps you brainstorm emotions and turn them into poetry. Start with "Emotional Clarity" in the center, then branch out to explore feelings, images, and inspirations for your next poem.

```
[Emotional Clarity]
    ├──── Core Emotions
    │       ├──── Happy (e.g., excited, content)
    │       ├──── Sad (e.g., lonely, hurt)
    │       ├──── Angry (e.g., frustrated, annoyed)
    │       └──── Afraid (e.g., anxious, scared)
    ├──── Images
    │       ├──── Nature (e.g., rain, sun)
    │       ├──── Objects (e.g., mirror, phone)
    │       ├──── Places (e.g., bedroom, park)
    │       └──── Actions (e.g., running, dancing)
    ├──── Inspirations
    │       ├──── Music (e.g., favorite playlist)
    │       ├──── Memories (e.g., a happy day)
    │       ├──── People (e.g., best friend)
    │       └──── Dreams (e.g., future goals)
    └──── Writing Goals
            ├──── Name the feeling
            ├──── Create one image
            ├──── Write for 5 minutes
            └──── Try a new prompt
```

Example Poem Using Mind Map (Core Emotion: Sad, Image: Rain, Inspiration: Memory, Goal: Name the feeling):

Sadness falls like rain on my roof,
A memory of loss, a quiet truth.
My pen names the ache, sets it free,
This page holds the heart of me.

Use this mind map to plan your next poem. Pick one idea from each branch and write for 5–10 minutes. Homeschoolers, this is a great tool for emotional reflection and creative writing.

🎯 ACTIVITY ZONE

ACTIVITY 1 – ANALYZING EMOTIONAL TONE

Read this poem by Mia, a 15-year-old from California:

My mood is a thunderstorm, dark and loud,
Anger flashes, a stormy cloud.
My pen strikes like lightning's spark,
Words clear the chaos in my heart.

1) What is the core emotion in Mia's poem?
a) Happy
b) Sad
c) Angry
d) Afraid

2) What specific feeling from the Emotion Wheel is present?
a) Content
b) Frustrated
c) Lonely
d) Excited

3) True or False: Mia's poem uses a weather metaphor.

4) Which prompt from the Mood Magic table did Mia likely use?
a) "When I felt this, I…"
b) "My mood is a…"
c) "Deep inside, I hide…"
d) "Someday, I'll feel…"

4) Which line shows writing helping Mia?
a) My mood is a thunderstorm, dark and loud
b) Anger flashes, a stormy cloud
c) My pen strikes like lightning's spark
d) Words clear the chaos in my heart

🎯 ACTIVITY ZONE

ACTIVITY 2 – IDENTIFYING SPECIFIC EMOTIONS

Read this poem by Noah, a 16-year-old from Texas:

This place holds my calm, a soft breeze,
Content like waves on quiet seas.
My words flow gently, steady, clear,
Peace lives here, no trace of fear.

1) What core emotion does Noah focus on?
a) Happy
b) Sad
c) Angry
d) Afraid

2) What specific feeling from the Emotion Wheel is present?
a) Excited
b) Content
c) Lonely
d) Scared

3) True or False: Noah's poem uses nature imagery.

4) Which prompt from the Mood Magic table did Noah likely use?
a) "My mood is a..."
b) "Deep inside, I hide..."
c) "This place holds my..."
d) "Someday, I'll feel..."

5) Which line shows Noah's sense of peace?
   1. a) This place holds my calm, a soft breeze
   2. b) Content like waves on quiet seas
   3. c) My words flow gently, steady, clear
   4. d) Peace lives here, no trace of fear

🎯 ACTIVITY ZONE
ACTIVITY 3 – SPOTTING POETIC DEVICES

Read this poem by Aisha, a 14-year-old from New York:

When I felt joy, I soared like a kite,
Colors bursting in the warm sunlight.
My heart danced, my pen flew free,
This page holds my happy spree.

1) What core emotion does Aisha focus on?
a) Sad
b) Happy
c) Angry
d) Afraid

2) What specific feeling from the Emotion Wheel is present?
a) Excited
b) Nervous
c) Hurt
d) Frustrated

3) True or False: Aisha's poem uses a simile to describe joy.

4) Which prompt from the Mood Magic table did Aisha likely use?
a) "When I felt this, I…"
b) "My mood is a…"
c) "This place holds my…"
d) "Deep inside, I hide…"

5) Which line shows Aisha's joy through action?
a) When I felt joy, I soared like a kite
b) Colors bursting in the warm sunlight
c) My heart danced, my pen flew free
d) This page holds my happy spree

🎯 ACTIVITY ZONE

ACTIVITY 4 – UNDERSTANDING EMOTIONAL IMPACT

Read this poem by Liam, a 17-year-old from Arizona:

Deep inside, I hide a quiet fear,
A shadow creeping, cold and near.
My words build a bridge to brighter days,
Fear fades in my poem's soft rays.

2) What core emotion does Liam focus on?
a) Happy
b) Sad
c) Angry
d) Afraid

2) What specific feeling from the Emotion Wheel is present?
a) Anxious
b) Proud
c) Annoyed
d) Content

3) True or False: Liam's poem suggests writing helps him cope.

4) Which prompt from the Mood Magic table did Liam likely use?
a) "My mood is a..."
b) "Deep inside, I hide..."
c) "This place holds my..."
d) "Someday, I'll feel..."

5) What image represents Liam's fear?
a) A stormy cloud
b) A shadow creeping
c) A sunny hill
d) A rising sun

ANSWERS
ACTIVITY ZONE

ACTIVITY 1 – ANALYZING EMOTIONAL TONE

1. c) Angry
2. b) Frustrated
3. True
4. b) "My mood is a…"
5. d) Words clear the chaos in my heart

ACTIVITY 2 – IDENTIFYING SPECIFIC EMOTIONS

1. a) Happy
2. b) Content
3. True
4. c) "This place holds my…"
5. d) Peace lives here, no trace of fear

ACTIVITY 3 – SPOTTING POETIC DEVICES

1. b) Happy
2. a) Excited
3. True
4. a) "When I felt this, I…"
5. c) My heart danced, my pen flew free

ACTIVITY 4 – UNDERSTANDING EMOTIONAL IMPACT

1. d) Afraid
2. a) Anxious
3. True
4. b) "Deep inside, I hide…"
5. b) A shadow creeping

Chapter 4. Who You Are: Identity in Verse

CHAPTER 4 – Who You Are: Identity in Verse

Learning Objectives:

In this chapter, you'll learn to express your identity through poetry by exploring your passions, culture, personality, and dreams using prompts, examples, and creative tools. You'll discover how to write poems that celebrate who you are and build confidence in your unique voice.

Hey, incredible teen! Ready to write poems that shout, "This is me!"? This chapter is all about exploring you—your quirks, your roots, your passions, and your dreams—through the power of poetry. Your identity is like your favorite playlist: one-of-a-kind and totally awesome. We'll help you craft verses that celebrate what makes you you, with tables, examples, prompts, an identity map, and fun activities with closed-ended questions. Whether you're writing for yourself, school, or to share on Instagram, this chapter will help you embrace your identity with confidence. Let's get started!

Using Poetry to Explore Your Identity

Who are you? It's a big question, and as a teen, you're figuring it out every day through your hobbies, your family, your friends, and your big dreams. Poetry is like a mirror that reflects your true self, letting you explore your identity in a creative, no-judgment zone. Whether you're the gamer, the poet, the shy artist, or the bold leader, your poems can capture what makes you unique.

Why is this so important? Writing about your identity builds self-awareness and confidence, key parts of social-emotional learning (SEL) in U.S. school curricula, according to the National Council of Teachers of English (NCTE). It also sharpens your narrative writing skills for essays, college applications, and tests like the SAT or ACT. Think of poets like Amanda Gorman, who celebrates her identity with bold words, or Walt Whitman, who wrote, "I am large, I contain multitudes." You've got multitudes too! Teachers, this chapter aligns with Common Core standards for narrative writing. Parents and homeschoolers, it's a perfect Q4 gift to spark self-discovery and creativity in teens. Want to share your work? Post with #IdentityInVerse to join a community of teen poets discovering themselves through writing!

Table: Why Identity Poetry Shines

Benefit	How It Helps	Example
Self-Awareness	Helps you understand who you are	A poem about your cultural heritage
Confidence	Celebrates your unique traits	Writing about your favorite hobby
Academic Success	Improves narrative writing skills	Using personal details in an essay
Connection	Shares your story with others	Posting a poem with #IdentityInVerse

Example: Here's a poem by Sofia, a 15-year-old from Florida:

I'm the spark in my sketchbook's lines,
Colors dancing where my heart shines.
My pen draws the me I want to be.

Sofia said, "This poem made me proud to be an artist." Let's write poems that celebrate you!

I Am: Defining Yourself

Your identity is a vibrant mix of your traits, passions, and experiences. Are you the kid who loves K-pop, the one who's always making TikToks, or the one dreaming of NASA? Poetry lets you define yourself on your own terms. Start by thinking about what makes you you—your hobbies, culture, or even your favorite food.

Example: Here's a poem by Carlos, a 16-year-old from New York, about his Puerto Rican roots:

I am the beat in my abuela's salsa,
Island sun in my heart's pulse.
My words carry her love's warm glow.

Table: Defining Your Identity

Category	Questions to Ask	Poem Idea
Passions	What do I love to do?	A poem about skateboarding
Culture	What traditions shape me?	A poem about a family recipe
Traits	What's my personality like?	A poem about being funny or quiet
Dreams	What do I hope to become?	A poem about a future career

Poetry as Your Mirror

Poetry reflects your truth, even the parts you keep hidden. You don't need to hide or polish anything—just write what feels real. Whether it's your culture, your struggles, or your proudest moments, your poems can capture the you that makes you special.

If you find more than one subject and verb in a sentence with no punctuation—🚨 It's likely a run-on!

Table: Reflecting Your Truth

Challenge	Truth	Action
"I don't know who I am."	You're figuring it out, and that's okay.	Write one line about how you feel today.
"My story's not exciting."	Every story is unique.	Write about a small moment, like a fun memory.
"I'm scared to be honest."	Poetry is a safe space.	Start with a private poem.
"It won't sound cool."	Your truth is always cool.	Write about something you love, even if it's "weird."

Prompt Practice: Your Story in Verse

Let's write! These five prompts are designed to help you tell your personal story through poetry. They're fun, teen-friendly, and perfect for exploring your identity. Write for 5–10 minutes per prompt, and let your truth shine—no pressure, just you.

5 Identity Prompts

Prompt #	Title	Kickoff Line	Example Line
1	*I Am Me*	"I am the…"	I am the rhythm in my dance moves.
2	*My Roots*	"My roots grow from…"	My roots grow from Mom's Sunday dinners.
3	*My Passion*	"This is where I shine…"	This is where I shine, on the basketball court.
4	*My Secret Self*	"No one knows I'm…"	No one knows I'm a writer of dreams.
5	*My Future Self*	"One day, I'll be…"	One day, I'll be coding my own app.

Example Poem (Prompt 2):

My roots grow from Abuela's stories,
Salsa beats and island glories.
My words carry her love's warm light,
This page holds my heritage bright.

How to Use: Pick one prompt, set a timer for 10 minutes, and write. If you're stuck, use the Identity Map below. Teachers, these prompts are great for narrative writing assignments. Parents, they're perfect for sparking self-discovery.

Visual Tool: Identity Map

Identity map helps you brainstorm what makes you you and turn it into poetry. Start with "You" in the center, then branch out to explore your family, friends, hobbies, and dreams.

```
[You]
├── Family
│   ├── Traditions (e.g., holiday meals)
│   ├── People (e.g., parents, siblings)
│   └── Culture (e.g., heritage, values)
├── Friends
│   ├── Besties (e.g., who you vibe with)
│   ├── Memories (e.g., late-night chats)
│   └── Support (e.g., who lifts you up)
├── Hobbies
│   ├── Passions (e.g., gaming, art)
│   ├── Skills (e.g., drawing, sports)
│   └── Fun (e.g., what makes you smile)
└── Dreams
    ├── Goals (e.g., college, career)
    ├── Adventures (e.g., travel, projects)
    └── Future Self (e.g., who you'll become)
```

Example Poem Using Identity Map (Family: Culture, Friends: Memories, Hobbies: Art, Dreams: Artist):

My roots are spiced with Mom's curry,
Friends' laughter echoes in my story.
My brush paints dreams of a gallery's light,
This page holds my heart's bright fight.

Use this map to plan your next poem. Pick one idea from each branch and write for 5–10 minutes. Homeschoolers, this is a great tool for self-reflection and narrative writing.

Example Poem Using Mind Map (Family: Values, Friends: Memories, Hobbies: Gaming, Dreams: Travel):

Kindness flows from Dad's old tales,
Friends' late-night laughs, where memory sails.
My controller hums, my dreams take flight,
One day, I'll roam beneath starlight.

Kindness flows from Dad's old tales,
Friends' late-night laughs, where memory sails.
My controller hums, my dreams take flight,
One day, I'll roam beneath starlight.

Your Turn: Reflective Journal Page

Take a moment to explore yourself! Use the blank identity map below to brainstorm, then try one of these prompts to write a poem. Check the box when you're done!

Blank Identity Map

```
[You]
    ├── Family
    │    ├── Traditions: _____
    │    ├── People: _____
    │    ├── Culture: _____
    ├── Friends
    │    ├── Besties: _____
    │    ├── Memories: _____
    │    ├── Support: _____
    ├── Hobbies
    │    ├── Passions: _____
    │    ├── Skills: _____
    │    ├── Fun: _____
    └── Dreams
         ├── Goals: _____
         ├── Adventures: _____
         └── Future Self: _____
```

Prompt Checkboxes

☐ Write a 4-line poem about a hidden part of yourself.
☐ Use your Identity Map to write a poem about your dreams.
☐ Share a line from your poem with a friend or post it with #IdentityInVerse.

How to Use: Fill out the blank identity map in your journal, then pick a prompt and write. Share your work with #IdentityInVerse to join a community of teen poets!

Sample Poems

Poem 1: Hidden Part of Myself

Inside my heart, a quiet dream takes wing,
A hope that grows with every step I tread.
I hide it softly, but it longs to sing,
A light that guides me to the days ahead.

Poem 2: Another Hidden Part

Beneath my smile, a spark of joy resides,
A wish to paint the world with colors bold.
I keep it tucked, but soon it won't abide,
My heart's bright fire will shine for all to hold.

Poem 3: Hidden Dreams

Deep in my soul, a vision glows with cheer,
A future bright where I can freely soar.
I guard it now, but soon I'll make it clear,
My dreams will bloom and open every door.

ACTIVITY ZONE
ACTIVITY 1: ANALYZING IDENTITY ELEMENTS

Read this poem by Mia, a 15-year-old from California:

I am the rhythm in my dance moves,
Feet tapping to my heart's grooves.
My pen spins my story, wild and free,
This page holds the truest me.

1) What part of Mia's identity is in the poem?
a) Her love for cooking
b) Her passion for dancing
c) Her family traditions
d) Her school achievements

2) What branch from the Identity Map does Mia focus on?
a) Family
b) Friends
c) Hobbies
d) Dreams

3) True or False: Mia's poem uses musical imagery.

4) Which prompt from the Your Story in Verse table did Mia likely use?
a) "I am the..."
b) "My roots grow from..."
c) "This is where I shine..."
d) "No one knows I'm..."

5) Which line shows Mia's sense of self?
a) I am the rhythm in my dance moves
b) Feet tapping to my heart's own grooves
c) My pen spins my story, wild and free
d) This page holds the truest me

ACTIVITY ZONE
ACTIVITY 2: IDENTIFYING CULTURAL ROOTS

Read this poem by Jayden, a 16-year-old from Texas:

My roots grow from Sunday dinners' glow,
Soul food stories only we know.
My words weave love from long ago,
This page holds my family's flow.

1) What part of Jayden's identity is in the poem?
a) His love for sports
b) His cultural heritage
c) His best friends
d) His future dreams

2) What branch from the Identity Map does Jayden focus on?
a) Family
b) Friends
c) Hobbies
d) Dreams

3) True or False: Jayden's poem mentions family traditions.

4) Which prompt from the Your Story in Verse table did Jayden likely use?
a) "I am the..."
b) "My roots grow from..."
c) "No one knows I'm..."
d) "One day, I'll be..."

5) Which line reflects Jayden's cultural pride?
a) My roots grow from Sunday dinners' glow
b) Soul food stories only we know
c) My words weave love from long ago
d) This page holds my family's flow

ACTIVITY ZONE
ACTIVITY 3: SPOTTING PERSONAL PASSION

Read this poem by Aisha, a 14-year-old from Chicago:

This is where I shine, on the basketball court,
Dribbling dreams where my heart's been caught.
My pen slams dunks no one can see,
This page is where I'm truly me.

1) What part of Aisha's identity is in the poem?
a) Her family traditions
b) Her passion for basketball
c) Her quiet personality
d) Her school achievements

2) What branch from the Identity Map does Aisha focus on?
a) Family
b) Friends
c) Hobbies
d) Dreams

3) True or False: Aisha's poem uses a sports metaphor.

4) Which prompt from the Your Story in Verse table did Aisha likely use?
a) "I am the…"
b) "My roots grow from…"
c) "This is where I shine…"
d) "No one knows I'm…"

5) Which line shows Aisha's passion?
a) This is where I shine, on the basketball court
b) Dribbling dreams where my heart's been caught
c) My pen slams dunks no one can see
d) This page is where I'm truly me

🎯 ACTIVITY ZONE
ACTIVITY 4: EXPLORING HIDDEN IDENTITY

Read this poem by Noah, a 17-year-old from Oregon:

No one knows I'm a coder of worlds,
Building dreams where code unfurls.
My pen crafts a future just for me,
This page holds my secret destiny.

1) What part of Noah's identity is in the poem?
a) His love for music
b) His hidden dreams
c) His family roots
d) His friendships

2) What branch from the Identity Map does Noah focus on?
a) Family
b) Friends
c) Hobbies
d) Dreams

3) True or False: Noah's poem uses technological imagery.

4) Which prompt from the Your Story in Verse table did Noah likely use?
a) "I am the..."
b) "My roots grow from..."
c) "This is where I shine..."
d) "No one knows I'm..."

5) Which line shows Noah's hidden self?
a) No one knows I'm a coder of worlds
b) Building dreams where code unfurls
c) My pen crafts a future just for me
d) This page holds my secret destiny

ANSWERS
🎯 ACTIVITY ZONE

ACTIVITY 1 – ANALYZING IDENTITY ELEMENTS

1. b) Her passion for dancing
2. c) Hobbies
3. True
4. a) "I am the…"
5. d) This page holds the truest me

ACTIVITY 2 – IDENTIFYING CULTURAL ROOTS

1. b) His cultural heritage
2. a) Family
3. True
4. b) "My roots grow from…"
5. d) This page holds my family's flow

ACTIVITY 3 – SPOTTING PERSONAL PASSION

1. b) Her passion for basketball
2. c) Hobbies
3. True
4. c) "This is where I shine…"
5. a) This is where I shine, on the basketball court

ACTIVITY 4 – EXPLORING HIDDEN IDENTITY

1. b) His hidden dreams
2. d) Dreams
3. True
4. d) "No one knows I'm…"
5. a) No one knows I'm a coder of worlds

Chapter 5. Crafting Aesthetic Vibes in Poetry

CHAPTER 5 – Crafting Aesthetic Vibes in Poetry

Learning Objectives:

You'll learn to write poems that pop with style and mood using vivid word choice, epic imagery, and aesthetic-inspired prompts. Create verses that feel like you—perfect for journaling, class, or sharing on Insta!

Hey, awesome teen! Ready to make your poems vibe like your favorite TikTok edit or Pinterest board? This chapter is all about crafting poetry that's bursting with aesthetic—think neon nights, cozy cafés, or dreamy sunsets. Whether you're into soft pastels or gritty urban feels, your words can capture your unique style. With tables, examples, prompts, a mood board, a mind map, and fun activities, you'll write poems that slay. Snap a pic of your poem with aesthetic objects and share it with #AestheticPoetry to join other teen poets! Let's make your words pop!

Introduction: Making Poems Pop with Style and Mood

Poetry is your vibe in words. Love the glow of fairy lights or the edge of a city street? Aesthetic poetry turns those feelings into a mini-movie in your reader's head. You're already a pro at curating vibes—your outfits, playlists, and posts scream you. Now, let's do that with poetry!

Why's this a big deal? Crafting aesthetic poems enhances your descriptive writing skills, aligning with school curricula for creative expression. It also helps you ace essays or tests like the SAT or ACT.

 Think of poets like Sylvia Plath, who painted moody vibes, or Ocean Vuong, whose words glow with feeling. You've got that spark, too! Teachers, this chapter supports Common Core standards for descriptive writing. Parents and homeschoolers, it's a perfect holiday gift to ignite teen creativity. Share your poems with #AestheticPoetry to vibe with other young poets!

Table: Why Aesthetic Poetry Slays

Benefit	How It Helps	Example
Creativity	Turns words into vivid vibes	A poem about a neon city
Expression	Shows off your unique style	Writing a cozy café poem
Academic Success	Boosts descriptive writing	Using imagery in essays
Connection	Shares your vibe with others	Posting with #AestheticPoetry

Example: Here's a poem by Mia, a 15-year-old from California:

Golden hour drips like honey slow,
Pastel skies where my dreams glow.
My words catch my heart's soft light.

Mia said, "This felt like capturing my favorite sunset." Ready to create your vibe? Let's go!

Setting the Tone

Tone is the vibe of your poem—dreamy, gritty, cozy, or bold. Your word choice is like picking the perfect filter for your Insta story. Choose words that match the mood you want to set, and your poem will hit just right.

Table: Setting the Tone

Tone	Mood It Creates	Word Choice
⭐ Dreamy	Soft, ethereal	Whisper, glow, haze
🔥 Gritty	Raw, intense	Grind, rust, pulse
☕ Cozy	Warm, comforting	Snug, flicker, wrap
⚡ Bold	Confident, vibrant	Crash, blaze, shout

🛠️ **Quick Craft Tip:**

Tone is the feeling your poem gives off, like a song's vibe. Pick words that match your mood to make it pop!
Example: Here's a poem by Jayden, a 16-year-old from Texas, using a cozy tone:

Snug in my hoodie, the fire's flicker,
Warmth wraps me, time ticks slower.
My pen hums a soft, cozy tune.

Try this: Pick a tone from the table on page [insert page number], choose two words, and write a 4-line poem. Teachers, this aligns with descriptive writing standards. Parents, it's a fun way to spark creativity.

Imagery That Shines

Imagery is the magic trick—it turns your poem into a mini-movie in your reader's head. Use colors, textures, and senses (sight, sound, touch, and smell) to bring your vibe to life. Think of your favorite aesthetic: what do you see, hear, or feel?

🎨 **Table: Imagery That Shines**

Sense	Example	Poem Idea
👁 Sight	Neon lights, velvet dusk	A poem about a city night
🔊 Sound	Rustling leaves, bass thrum	A poem about a forest vibe
✋ Touch	Soft moss, gritty pavement	A poem about a favorite spot
👃 Smell	Fresh rain, coffee beans	A poem about a morning mood

Prompt Practice: Your Story in Verse

🔧 **Quick Craft Tip**: Imagery uses the five senses to paint a picture. Try adding one sensory detail (like "gritty pavement") to make your poem vivid!
Example: Here's a poem by Aisha, a 14-year-old from Chicago, using sight and smell:

Neon lights buzz, rain's fresh scent,
City nights are where my heart's spent.
My words paint a street's electric spark.

Try it: Pick a sense from the table, choose an example, and write a 4-line poem. Homeschoolers, this builds sensory detail skills, perfect for SEL and creative writing.

Prompt Practice: Visual Poetry

Time to write some aesthetic magic! These five prompts are all about creating poems that burst with style and vibe. They're teen-friendly and perfect for capturing your aesthetic. Write for 5–10 minutes per prompt, and let your imagination run wild. Snap a pic of your poem with aesthetic objects (like a candle or your favorite hoodie) and share it with #AestheticPoetry!

✎ **Table: Visual Poetry Prompts**

Prompt #	Title	Kickoff Line	Example Line
1	My Vibe	"My world glows like…"	My world glows like a starry dusk.
2	Sensory Snapshot	"I hear, I see, I feel…"	I hear rain, I see mist, I feel calm.
3	Color Story	"This color paints my…"	This gold paints my hopeful heart.
4	Place Vibes	"This place feels like…"	This park feels like a green escape.
5	Dream Aesthetic	"In my dream world…"	In my dream world, neon lights dance.

🎧 Aesthetic Playlist – Dreamy

- "Daylight" by Taylor Swift
- "Electric Feel" by MGMT
- "Space Song" by Beach House

Example Poem (Prompt 4):

This café feels like a warm hug,
Coffee's scent in a cozy mug.
My words brew soft, like morning light,
This page holds my heart's delight.

How to Use: Pick one prompt from the table on page [insert page number], set a timer for 10 minutes, and write. Stuck? Check out the Aesthetic Mood Board Table below. ⚡ Challenge Yourself: Turn your 4-line poem into a haiku or a free verse poem with two stanzas. Teachers, these prompts are perfect for descriptive writing assignments. Parents, they're great for sparking creative vibes.

Visual Tool: Aesthetic Mood Board Table

This table helps you craft aesthetic poetry. Select a mood, then use the colors, textures, and words to evoke your desired vibe.

Mood	Colors	Textures	Sample Words
Dreamy	Pastel pink, lavender	Silk, clouds	Whisper, haze, drift
🔥 Gritty	Charcoal, neon red	Rust, concrete	Grind, pulse, clash
☕ Cozy	Warm brown, gold	Wool, velvet	Snug, flicker, warm
⚡ Bold	Electric blue, lime	Glass, metal	Blaze, shout, spark

Example Poem Using Mood Board (Mood: Gritty, Colors: Neon red, Texture: Concrete, Words: Pulse):

Neon red pulses on concrete streets,
City's heartbeat where my soul meets.
My pen scratches a gritty, raw spark,
This page holds my urban heart.

Use this table to plan your poem. Pick a mood, mix in colors and textures, and write for 5–10 minutes. Refer to page [insert page number] to review the table. Homeschoolers, this is a dope tool for descriptive writing.

Your Turn: Reflective Journal Page

Create your aesthetic vibe! Fill out the blank mood board below, then pick a prompt to write a poem. Check the box when you're done!

Blank Aesthetic Mood Board

Mood	Colors	Textures	Sample Words
___	___	___	___
___	___	___	___
___	___	___	___
___	___	___	___

Prompt Checkboxes

☐ Write a 4-line poem about a cozy vibe.
☐ Use your Mood Board to write a poem about a color.
☐ Snap a pic of your poem with aesthetic objects (like your favorite mug) and post with #AestheticPoetry.

How to Use: Fill out the mood board in your journal, pick a prompt, and write. Share your vibe with #AestheticPoetry to join other teen poets!

Visual Tool: Aesthetic Vibe Mind Map

This mind map helps you brainstorm aesthetic vibes for your poetry. Start with "Aesthetic Vibes" in the center, then branch out to create your poem.

```
[Aesthetic Vibes]
    ├── Moods
    │    ├── 💭 Dreamy (e.g., pastel, soft)
    │    ├── 🔥 Gritty (e.g., urban, raw)
    │    ├── ☕ Cozy (e.g., warm, snug)
    │    └── ⚡ Bold (e.g., vibrant, loud)
    ├── Senses
    │    ├── 👁 Sight (e.g., neon, dusk)
    │    ├── 🔊 Sound (e.g., waves, bass)
    │    ├── ✋ Touch (e.g., silk, concrete)
    │    └── 👃 Smell (e.g., rain, coffee)
    ├── Inspirations
    │    ├── Places (e.g., café, city)
    │    ├── Music (e.g., lo-fi, pop)
    │    ├── Colors (e.g., blue, gold)
    │    └── Vibes (e.g., retro, modern)
    └── Writing Goals
         ├── Set a tone
         ├── Use one sense
         ├── Try a new prompt
         └── Paint a vivid image
```

Example Poem Using Mind Map (Mood: Bold, Sense: Sight, Inspiration: City, Goal: Paint a vivid image):

Electric blue lights blaze the night,
City's pulse in my heart's bright fight.
My pen sparks a vibrant, wild mark.

Use this mind map on the page to plan your poem. Pick one idea from each branch and write for 5–10 minutes. Homeschoolers, this is a dope tool for creative writing.

60

🎯 ACTIVITY ZONE

ACTIVITY 1 – ANALYZING AESTHETIC TONE

Read this poem by Liam, a 15-year-old from California:

My world glows like a starry dusk,
Lavender haze where dreams don't rust.
My pen weaves a soft, cosmic stream.

1) What tone does Liam's poem create?
a) Gritty
b) Dreamy
c) Cozy
d) Bold

2) What color from the Aesthetic Mood Board is used?
a) Neon red
b) Lavender
c) Warm brown
d) Electric blue

3) True or False: Liam's poem uses a dreamy mood.

4) Which prompt from the Visual Poetry table did Liam likely use?
a) "My world glows like…"
b) "I hear, I see, I feel…"
c) "This color paints my…"
d) "This place feels like…"

5) Which line sets the aesthetic tone?
a) My world glows like a starry dusk
b) Lavender haze where dreams don't rust
c) My pen weaves a soft, cosmic stream
d) All of the above

ACTIVITY 2 – IDENTIFYING SENSORY IMAGERY

Read this poem by Sofia, a 16-year-old from Texas:

I hear rain, I see mist, I feel calm,
Forest's hush in my heart's soft palm.
My words paint a green, quiet song.

1) What sense is most prominent in Sofia's poem?
a) Sight
b) Sound
c) Touch
d) All of the above

2) What texture from the Aesthetic Mood Board is implied?
a) Silk
b) Concrete
c) Wool
d) Clouds

3) True or False: Sofia's poem uses multiple senses.

4) Which prompt from the Visual Poetry table did Sofia likely use?
a) "My world glows like…"
b) "I hear, I see, I feel…"
c) "This color paints my…"
d) "In my dream world…"

5) Which line includes sensory imagery?
a) I hear rain, I see mist, I feel calm
b) Forest's hush in my heart's soft palm
c) My words paint a green, quiet song
d) All of the above

ACTIVITY 3 – SPOTTING COLOR AND MOOD

Read this poem by Noah, a 14-year-old from Illinois:

*This gold paints my hopeful heart,
Like sunlight beams that never part.
My pen flows bold, a radiant stream.*

1) What mood does Noah's poem create?
a) Gritty
b) Dreamy
c) Cozy
d) Bold

2) What color from the Aesthetic Mood Board is used?
a) Pastel pink
b) Gold
c) Charcoal
d) Lavender

3) True or False: Noah's poem uses light imagery.

4) Which prompt from the Visual Poetry table did Noah likely use?
a) "My world glows like…"
b) "I hear, I see, I feel…"
c) "This color paints my…"
d) "This place feels like…"

5) Which line sets the mood?
a) This gold paints my hopeful heart
b) Like sunlight beams that never part
c) My pen flows bold, a radiant stream
d) All of the above

ACTIVITY 4 – EXPLORING PLACE VIBES

Read this poem by Carlos, a 17-year-old from Florida:

This park feels like a green escape,
Rustling leaves shape my heart's landscape.
My words grow soft, like morning dew.

1) What mood does Carlos's poem create?
a) Gritty
b) Dreamy
c) Cozy
d) Bold

2) What texture from the Aesthetic Mood Board is implied?
a) Concrete
b) Velvet
c) Silk
d) Clouds

3) True or False: Carlos's poem uses nature imagery.

4) Which prompt from the Visual Poetry table did Carlos likely use?
a) "My world glows like…"
b) "I hear, I see, I feel…"
c) "This color paints my…"
d) "This place feels like…"

5) Which line sets the aesthetic vibe?
a) This park feels like a green escape
b) Rustling leaves shape my heart's landscape
c) My words grow soft, like morning dew
d) All of the above

ANSWERS
🎯 ACTIVITY ZONE

ACTIVITY 1 – ANALYZING AESTHETIC TONE

1. b) Dreamy
2. b) Lavender
3. True
4. a) "My world glows like…"
5. a) My world glows like a starry dusk

ACTIVITY 2 – IDENTIFYING SENSORY IMAGERY

1. d) All of the above
2. d) Clouds
3. True
4. b) "I hear, I see, I feel…"
5. d) All of the above

ACTIVITY 3 – SPOTTING COLOR AND MOOD

1. d) Bold
2. b) Gold
3. True
4. c) "This color paints my…"
5. a) This gold paints my hopeful heart

ACTIVITY 4 – EXPLORING PLACE VIBES

1. b) Dreamy
2. d) Clouds
3. True
4. d) "This place feels like…"
5. a) This park feels like a green escape

Peer Review Quick Guide

Share your poem with a friend or classmate! Use this checklist to give feedback:

- ⊘ Does the poem create a strong vibe?
- ⊘ Can I see or feel the imagery?
- ⊘ Do the words match the mood?
- ⊘ Is there a clear tone or style?

Chapter 6. Poems for Friends, Family, and Feels

66

CHAPTER 6 – Poems for Friends, Family, and Feels

Learning Objectives:

You'll be able to write heartfelt poems that celebrate your connections with friends, family, or crushes and process big emotions using vivid letter-style poems, a relationship web, and fun activities.

Hey, epic teen! Your friends, family, and maybe even a crush—they're the heartbeat of your life. This chapter is all about writing poems that vibe with those connections, whether you're hyping up your bestie or sorting through family feels. Poetry is like a DM from your heart, capturing love, fights, and everything in between. With tables, diverse examples, prompts, a relationship web, and activities, you'll craft poems that feel you. Snap a pic of your poem with something special (like a family photo) and share it with #HeartfeltPoetry to join other teen poets. Let's spill those feels on the page!

Introduction: Poetry for the People You Love

Your squad, your family, that special someone—they shape who you are. Poetry lets you celebrate those bonds or work through the messy moments, like a fight with a friend or a family misunderstanding. It's a safe way to say what's in your heart, whether it's love, regret, or hope.

Why write about relationships? It builds empathy and emotional smarts, key parts of social-emotional learning (SEL) in U.S. schools, aligning with Common Core standards for narrative writing (CCSS.ELA-LITERACY.W.9-10.3). It also preps you for essays or tests like the SAT or ACT. Think of poets like Maya Angelou, whose words hug you with love, or Pablo Neruda, who makes crushes feel magical. You've got that power too! Teachers, use this chapter for SEL or writing units. Parents and homeschoolers, it's a perfect holiday gift to spark a connection. Share your poems with #HeartfeltPoetry or create a Canva post to join a teen poetry vibe!

Table: Why Relationship Poetry Slays

Benefit	How It Helps	Example
Empathy	Understands others' feelings	A poem for a friend's tough day
Expression	Shares love or heals hurts	Writing about a family moment
Academic Success	Boosts narrative skills	Using relationships in essays
Connection	Bonds with others	Posting with #HeartfeltPoetry

Example: Here's a poem by Amara, 15, from Georgia:

My bestie's smile is my sunny day,
Her laugh chases my clouds away.
My words hold our bond, always near.

Amara said, "This poem was like texting my friend a hug." Let's write poems that light up your connections!

Celebrating Connections

Your friends, family, or chosen family are your vibe tribe. Poetry lets you hype them up like a shout-out on your story. Focus on what makes them special—your friend's goofy jokes, your tita's adobo, or your cousin's epic playlists.

👤 **How to Use This Table**: Pick a person and a trait to inspire a poem that celebrates them.

🛠 **Quick Craft Tip:** Use specific details (like "your loud laugh") to make your poem pop. Struggling? Try this starter: "You're the one who…"

Table: Celebrating Connections

Person	What to Highlight	Poem Idea
⭐ Friend	Laughs, loyalty	A poem about a group chat
👨‍👩‍👧 Parent/Chosen Family	Love, wisdom	A poem about a life lesson
👯 Sibling	Fun, rivalry	A poem about a shared game
💚 Special Someone	Kindness, vibe	A poem about a sweet moment

🛠 Quick Craft Tip:

Use specific details (like "your loud laugh") to make your poem pop. Struggling? Try this starter: "You're the one who…"
Scaffolded Example (Friend):

Idea: My friend Priya's loyalty
Brainstorm: Always there, late-night talks, trust
Draft: You're the one who stays when skies are gray…

Polished Poem (by Priya, 16, from California):

You're the one who stays when skies are gray,
Your loyalty's my light, my sunny ray.
My pen writes our friendship, bold and true.

Try this: Pick a person from the table on page [insert page number], highlight one trait, and write a 4-line poem. Teachers, this supports narrative writing (CCSS.ELA-LITERACY.W.9-10.3). Parents, it's a fun way to celebrate loved ones.

Healing Through Verse

Relationships can get messy—fights with friends or family drama can sting.

Poetry is your safe space to process those emotions and find peace. Write about the hurt, regret, or hope to heal your heart. Content Note: Writing about conflict can feel heavy—take your time and keep it private if needed.

How to Use This Table: Choose an emotion to express in a poem that heals or rebuilds.

💔 **Table: Healing Through Verse**

Emotion	What to Express	Poem Idea
😣 Hurt	Pain, betrayal	A poem about a friend's fight
😔 Regret	Wishing to fix things	A poem about saying sorry
💕 Love	Bonds despite conflict	A poem about family strength
🌈 Hope	Moving forward	A poem about rebuilding trust

🛠️ **Quick Craft Tip:** Use metaphors (like "my heart's a cracked mirror") to express tough feels. Struggling? Try this starter: "I feel…"

Scaffolded Example (Regret):
- Idea: Regret for yelling at my sister
- Brainstorm: Anger, guilt, wanting to fix it
- Draft: I feel the sting of my sharp words…

Polished Poem (by Diego, 14, from Texas):

I feel the sting of my sharp words' bite,
Regret's a shadow in my heart's light.
My pen builds a bridge to make us whole.

Try it: Pick an emotion from the table, use a metaphor, and write a 4-line poem. Homeschoolers, this builds SEL skills like emotional regulation.

Prompt Practice: Letter Poems

Time to write heartfelt letter-style poems to someone special—friend, family, crush, or chosen family. These five prompts are ideal for expressing love or working through emotions. Write for 5–10 minutes, and let your heart spill out. Create a poetry reel or record an audio reading and share with #HeartfeltPoetry!

✉ **How to Use This Table:** Pick a prompt, start with the kickoff line, and write a poem. Reflect: How did writing this make you feel? Would you share it with the person?

Letter Poem Prompts

Prompt #	Title	Kickoff Line	Example Line
1	To My Bestie	"Dear friend, you are…"	Dear friend, you are my loudest laugh.
2	To My Family	"Dear family, you hold…"	Dear family, you hold my deepest roots.
3	To My Crush	"Dear you, my heart…"	Dear you, my heart hums your quiet smile.
4	To Someone I Hurt	"Dear you, I'm sorry…"	Dear you, I'm sorry for my cold words.
5	To Someone I Miss	"Dear you, I miss…"	Dear you, I miss your warm embrace.

🎧 Heartfelt Playlist – Connection

- "Count on Me" by Bruno Mars
- "My Same" by Adele
- "Home" by Edward Sharpe & The Magnetic Zeros

Example Poem (Prompt 3):

Dear you, my heart hums at your quiet smile,
Like fireflies dancing for a while.
My words hold this crush, shy and sweet,
This page keeps our spark's gentle beat.
(By Linh, 17, from New York)

How to Use: Pick a prompt from the table on page [insert page number], set a timer for 10 minutes, and write. Stuck? Use the Relationship Web on page [insert page number] or try RhymeZone.com for rhyme ideas.

⚡ **Challenge Yourself:** Write from the other person's POV or turn your poem into a spoken word piece. Teachers, these prompts are great for narrative writing. Parents, they're perfect for emotional connection. Reflect: Would you share this poem?

Visual Tool: Relationship Web

This web helps you brainstorm poems about your relationships—friends, family, crushes, or chosen family. Start with "You" in the center, then connect to emotions and memories.

```
[You]
    ├──── 👥 Friends
    │      ├──── Emotions (e.g., joy, trust)
    │      ├──── Memories (e.g., group chats)
    │      └──── Moments (e.g., late-night laughs)
    ├──── 👨‍👩‍👧 Family/Chosen Family
    │      ├──── Emotions (e.g., love, pride)
    │      ├──── Memories (e.g., holiday dinners)
    │      └──── Moments (e.g., advice given)
    └──── 💜 Crushes
           ├──── Emotions (e.g., butterflies, hope)
           ├──── Memories (e.g., shared glances)
           └──── Moments (e.g., a kind gesture)
```

Your Turn: Fill This Out!

[You]
```
    ├── 👥 Friends
    │   ├── Emotions: _____
    │   ├── Memories: _____
    │   └── Moments: _____
    ├── 👨‍👩‍👧 Family/Chosen Family
    │   ├── Emotions: _____
    │   ├── Memories: _____
    │   └── Moments: _____
    └── 💗 Crushes
        ├── Emotions: _____
        ├── Memories: _____
        └── Moments: _____
```

Example Poem Using Relationship Web (Family: Pride, Memories: Holiday dinners, Moments: Advice):

Your pride's the glow of our Diwali nights,
Dad's advice is like lanterns burning bright.
My pen holds our love, forever true.
(By Anika, 16, from Illinois)

Use this web page to plan your poem. Pick one idea from each branch and write for 5–10 minutes. Homeschoolers, this is a dope tool for narrative writing.

Visual Tool: Relationship Connection Mind Map

[Insert visual diagram of a 4-branch mind map: Friends, Family/Chosen Family, Crushes, Writing Goals]

This mind map helps you brainstorm poems about your connections. Start with "Connections" in the center, then branch out to spark ideas.

```
[Connections]
    ├── 👥 Friends
    │   ├── Emotions (e.g., joy, trust)
    │   ├── Memories (e.g., group chats)
    │   ├── Moments (e.g., shared laughs)
    ├── 👨‍👩‍👧 Family/Chosen Family
    │   ├── Emotions (e.g., love, pride)
    │   ├── Memories (e.g., holiday dinners)
    │   ├── Moments (e.g., advice given)
    └── 💗 Crushes
        ├── Emotions (e.g., butterflies, hope)
        ├── Memories (e.g., shared glances)
        └── Writing Goals
            ├── Express a feeling
            ├── Capture a memory
            ├── Use a metaphor
            ├── Write a letter poem
```

Example Poem Using Mind Map (Crushes: Butterflies, Memories: Shared glances, Goal: Use a metaphor):

Your glance is a spark in my heart's night sky,
Butterflies dance where my dreams fly high.
My pen holds this crush, soft and true.
(By Aaliyah, 15, from Chicago)

Use this mind map on the page to plan your poem. Pick one idea from each branch and write for 5–10 minutes. Homeschoolers, this is a dope tool for narrative writing.

🎯 ACTIVITY ZONE

ACTIVITY 1 – ANALYZING FRIENDSHIP POEMS

Read this poem by Amara, 15, from Georgia:

Dear friend, you are my loudest laugh,
Our group chats spark my heart's true path.
My words weave our vibe, forever strong.

1) Who is Amara's poem addressed to?
a) A parent
b) A friend
c) A crush
d) A sibling

2) What moment from the Relationship Web is used?
a) Holiday dinners
b) Group chats
c) Shared glances
d) Advice given

3) True or False: Amara's poem uses laughter imagery.

4) Which prompt from the Letter Poem table did Amara likely use?
a) "Dear friend, you are…"
b) "Dear family, you hold…"
c) "Dear you, my heart…"
d) "Dear you, I'm sorry…"

5) Which line shows the friendship bond?
a) Dear friend, you are my loudest laugh
b) Our group chats spark my heart's true path
c) My words weave our vibe, forever strong
d) All of the above

ACTIVITY 2 –IDENTIFYING FAMILY CONNECTIONS

Read this poem by Diego, 14, from Texas:

Dear family, you hold my deepest roots,
Abuelo's stories, love in every truth.
My pen weaves our bond, warm and true.

1) Who is Diego's poem addressed to?
a) A friend
b) A family
c) A crush
d) A teacher

2) What memory from the Relationship Web is used?
a) Group chats
b) Holiday dinners
c) Stories
d) Late-night laughs

3) True or False: Diego's poem mentions family stories.

4) Which prompt from the Letter Poem table did Diego likely use?
a) "Dear friend, you are…"
b) "Dear family, you hold…"
c) "Dear you, I'm sorry…"
d) "Dear you, I miss…"

5) Which line highlights the family bond?
a) Dear family, you hold my deepest roots
b) Abuelo's stories, love in every truth
c) My pen weaves our bond, warm and true
d) All of the above

ACTIVITY 3 – SPOTTING EMOTIONAL HEALING

Read this poem by Linh, 17, from New York:

Dear you, I'm sorry for my cold words,
Like ice that cracked, they hurt, I've learned.
My pen mends our trust with gentle light.

1) What emotion is Linh expressing?
a) Joy
b) Regret
c) Love
d) Hope

2) What metaphor from the Healing Through Verse table is used?
a) Storm
b) Sun
c) Ice
d) Fireworks

3) True or False: Linh's poem focuses on healing a conflict.

4) Which prompt from the Letter Poem table did Linh likely use?
a) "Dear friend, you are…"
b) "Dear you, my heart…"
c) "Dear you, I'm sorry…"
d) "Dear you, I miss…"

5) Which line shows the healing intent?
a) Dear you, I'm sorry for my cold words
b) Like ice that cracked, they hurt, I've learned
c) My pen mends our trust with gentle light
d) All of the above

ACTIVITY 4 – ANALYZING CRUSH POEMS

Read this poem by Malik, 16, from Florida:

Dear you, my heart hums at your warm glance,
Like fireflies in a quiet dance.
My words hold this crush, shy and sweet.

1) Who is Malik's poem addressed to?
a) A friend
b) A family member
c) A crush
d) A sibling

2) What emotion from the Relationship Web is used?
a) Joy
b) Butterflies
c) Pride
d) Trust

3) True or False: Malik's poem uses nature imagery.

4) Which prompt from the Letter Poem table did Malik likely use?
a) "Dear friend, you are…"
b) "Dear family, you hold…"
c) "Dear you, my heart…"
d) "Dear you, I miss…"

5) Which line shows the crushed emotion?
a) Dear you, my heart hums at your warm glance
b) Like fireflies in a quiet dance
c) My words hold this crush, shy and sweet
d) All of the above

ANSWERS
ACTIVITY ZONE

ACTIVITY 1 – ANALYZING FRIENDSHIP POEMS

1. b) A friend
2. b) Group chats
3. True
4. a) "Dear friend, you are…"
5. c) My words weave our vibe, forever strong

ACTIVITY 2 – IDENTIFYING FAMILY CONNECTIONS

1. b) A family
2. c) Stories
3. True
4. b) "Dear family, you hold…"
5. d) All of the above

ACTIVITY 3 – SPOTTING EMOTIONAL HEALING

1. b) Regret
2. c) Ice
3. True
4. c) "Dear you, I'm sorry…"
5. c) My pen mends our trust with gentle light

ACTIVITY 4 – ANALYZING CRUSH POEMS

1. c) A crush
2. b) Butterflies
3. True
4. c) "Dear you, my heart…"
5. d) All of the above

Peer Review Quick Guide
Share your poem with a friend or classmate! Use this checklist to give feedback. Example: "Your poem's emotion is strong because 'sunny ray' feels so warm!"

- ⊘ Does the poem capture a strong emotion?
- ⊘ Can I feel the connection to the person?
- ⊘ Do the words reflect a specific memory or moment?
- ⊘ Is there a clear tone (e.g., loving, apologetic)?

Chapter 7. Holiday Vibes: Seasonal Poetry Prompts

CHAPTER 7 – Holiday Vibes: Seasonal Poetry Prompts

Hey, awesome teen! Q4 holidays are the vibe—twinkling lights, cozy gatherings, and all the feels. This chapter is your guide to writing poems that capture the magic of Christmas, Thanksgiving, or any winter celebration that lights up your heart. Whether you're hyping up snowy nights or giving thanks for your squad, your words can shine like a holiday star. With tables, diverse examples, prompts, a holiday planner, and fun activities, you'll craft poems that pop. Snap a pic of your poem with festive vibes (like a holiday mug) and share it with #HolidayPoetryVibes to join other teen poets. Let's make your holiday feels glow on the page!

Capturing Holiday Magic in Verse

Holidays like Christmas and Thanksgiving bring cozy moments, family traditions, and big emotions—perfect for poetry! Whether it's the sparkle of Christmas lights or the warmth of a Thanksgiving table, your poems can bottle up that seasonal magic. Writing holiday poetry allows you to celebrate joy, reflect on gratitude, or even process the bittersweet feelings of the season.

Why's this a big deal? Holiday poetry boosts your narrative and descriptive writing skills, aligning with U.S. school curricula (Common Core, CCSS.ELA-LITERACY.W.9-10.3) and SEL goals like gratitude and reflection, per CASEL frameworks. It's also great for essays or tests, such as the SAT or ACT. Think of poets like Robert Frost, whose wintery words feel like a snowy night, or Langston Hughes, who celebrated community. You've got that spark, too! Teachers, use this chapter for holiday-themed writing or SEL units. Parents and homeschoolers, it's a perfect holiday gift to inspire festive creativity. Share your poems with #HolidayPoetryVibes or make a Canva post to vibe with other teens!

📚 **Teacher Tip:** Use this chapter for holiday writing projects or gratitude-focused SEL lessons.

Table: Why Holiday Poetry Slays

Prompt #	Title	Kickoff Line	Example Line
1	To My Bestie	"Dear friend, you are…"	Dear friend, you are my loudest laugh.
2	To My Family	"Dear family, you hold…"	Dear family, you hold my deepest roots.
3	To My Crush	"Dear you, my heart…"	Dear you, my heart hums your quiet smile.
4	To Someone I Hurt	"Dear you, I'm sorry…"	Dear you, I'm sorry for my cold words.
5	To Someone I Miss	"Dear you, I miss…"	Dear you, I miss your warm embrace.

Example: Here's a poem by Jaden, 15, from Colorado:

Snowflakes dance, my heart's aglow,
Christmas lights paint a wintry show.
My words catch this holiday's spark.

Jaden said, "This poem felt like wrapping up a snowy night." Ready to write your holiday vibe? Let's dive in!

Christmas and Winter Wonders

Christmas and winter holidays are all about sparkle—think twinkling lights, cozy fires, or Hanukkah candles. Poetry lets you capture that festive cheer, from family traditions to snowy dreams. Focus on what makes your winter holiday special, whether it's a cultural celebration or a quiet moment.

❄ How to Use This Table: Pick a holiday and vibe to inspire a poem full of winter magic.

🔨 **Quick Craft Tip**: Use sensory details (like "crisp snow crunch") to make your poem vivid. Struggling? Try this starter: "This holiday feels like…"

Scaffolded Example (Christmas):

- Idea: Decorating the Christmas tree
- Brainstorm: Lights, ornaments, family laughter
- Draft: This holiday feels like twinkling lights…
- Polished Poem (by Mia, 16, from Michigan):

This holiday feels like twinkling lights,
Ornaments glow in our family's nights.
My pen holds this Christmas joy so bright.

Try this: Pick a holiday from the table on page [insert page number], choose a vibe, and write a 4-line poem. Teachers, this supports descriptive writing (CCSS.ELA-LITERACY.W.9-10.3). Parents, it's a fun way to celebrate holiday traditions.

❄ Table: Christmas and Winter Wonders

Holiday	Vibe to Capture	Poem Idea
🎄 Christmas	Joy, warmth	A poem about decorating the tree
🕎 Hanukkah	Light, hope	A poem about lighting candles
❄ Winter Solstice	Quiet, renewal	A poem about a snowy night
🕯 Kwanzaa	Community, pride	A poem about a family gathering

Scaffolded Example (Christmas):

- Idea: Decorating the Christmas tree
- Brainstorm: Lights, ornaments, family laughter
- Draft: This holiday feels like twinkling lights…
- Polished Poem (by Mia, 16, from Michigan):

This holiday feels like twinkling lights,
Ornaments glow in our family's nights.
My pen holds this Christmas joy so bright.

Thanksgiving and Gratitude

Thanksgiving is all about giving thanks and reflecting on what matters—family, friends, or even small moments. Poetry helps you express gratitude or explore the deeper feelings of the season, like missing someone at the table. Write about what fills your heart with thanks.

🦃 How to Use This Table: Choose a gratitude focus to craft a poem that reflects your heart.

🦃 Table: Thanksgiving and Gratitude

Focus	What to Express	Poem Idea
👪 Family	Love, togetherness	A poem about a Thanksgiving meal
👫 Friends	Support, memories	A poem about a friend's kindness
⭐ Personal Growth	Strength, lessons	A poem about overcoming a challenge
🌸 Community	Belonging, care	A poem about a group moment

🔧 **Quick Craft Tip**: Use metaphors (like "gratitude's a warm fire") to deepen your poem. Struggling? Try this starter: "I'm thankful for…"

Scaffolded Example (Family):
- Idea: Thanksgiving dinner with family
- Brainstorm: Warmth, laughter, shared stories
- Draft: I'm thankful for our table's glow…
- Polished Poem (by Aaliyah, 14, from Georgia):

I'm thankful for our table's glow,
Family laughter like a river's flow.
My pen holds this gratitude so true.

Try it: Pick a focus from the table, use a metaphor, and write a 4-line poem. Homeschoolers, this builds SEL skills like gratitude and reflection.

Prompt Practice: Holiday Glow

Time to write festive poems that shine with holiday magic! These five prompts are perfect for capturing the glow of Q4 celebrations—Christmas, Thanksgiving, or any winter tradition. Write for 5-10 minutes, letting your holiday spirit flow. Create a poetry reel or record an audio reading and share with #HolidayPoetryVibes!

🧑‍🎄 **How to Use This Table:** Pick a prompt, start with the kickoff line, and write a poem. Reflect: How did writing this make you feel? Would you share it with someone?

Prompt #	Title	Kickoff Line	Example Line
1	Winter Night	"The winter night glows…"	The winter night glows with snowy dreams.
2	Holiday Tradition	"This tradition feels like…"	This tradition feels like a warm hug.
3	Gratitude Moment	"I'm thankful for this…"	I'm thankful for this table's love.
4	Festive Memory	"This holiday memory…"	This holiday memory sparkles bright.
5	Seasonal Wish	"My holiday wish is…"	My holiday wish is peace for all.

🎧 Holiday Playlist – Festive Vibes

- "Winter Song" by Sara Bareilles & Ingrid Michaelson
- "Grateful" by John Bucchino
- "This Christmas" by Donny Hathaway

Example Poem (Prompt 2):

This tradition feels like a warm hug,
Lighting candles on our Hanukkah rug.
My words hold this glow, soft and true.

(By Noah, 17, from New York)

Visual Tool: Holiday Prompt Planner

This table helps you craft festive poems. Pick a holiday, mood, or imagery to spark your writing.

🎄 Holiday Prompt Planner

Holiday	Mood	Imagery	Prompt Idea
🎄 Christmas	Joyful	Twinkling lights	A poem about a tree-lighting moment
🦃 Thanksgiving	Grateful	Warm table	A poem about a family dinner
🕎 Hanukkah	Hopeful	Candle glow	A poem about lighting the menorah
🕯 Kwanzaa	Proud	Unity cup	A poem about community values

Your Turn: Fill This Out!

Holiday	Mood	Imagery	Prompt Idea
_____	_____	_____	_____
_____	_____	_____	_____
_____	_____	_____	_____
_____	_____	_____	_____

Example Poem Using Planner (Holiday: Thanksgiving, Mood: Grateful, Imagery: Warm table):

Our table's warmth lights up my heart,
Gratitude's fire where love does start.
My pen holds this Thanksgiving glow.

(By Sofia, 16, from Texas)

Your Turn: Reflective Journal Page

Capture your holiday vibe in a poem! Fill out the blank holiday planner, then pick a prompt to write. Struggling? Try a fill-in-the-blank: "This holiday is my __." Check the box when done!

Your Turn: Fill This Out!

Holiday	Mood	Imagery	Prompt Idea
___	___	___	___
___	___	___	___
___	___	___	___
___	___	___	___

Prompt Checkboxes

☐ Write a 4-line poem about a winter holiday tradition.
☐ Use your Holiday Planner to write about a gratitude moment.
☐ Create a poetry reel with your poem and a festive object (like a holiday ornament) and post with #HolidayPoetryVibes.

How to Use: Fill out the planner in your journal, pick a prompt, and write. Reflect: How did writing this make you feel? Share with #HolidayPoetryVibes or on RhymeZone.com's forums!

Visual Tool: Holiday Connection Mind Map

This mind map helps you brainstorm festive poems. Start with "Holiday Vibes" in the center, then branch out to spark ideas.

```
[Holiday Vibes]
    ├── 🎄 Holidays
    │   ├── Christmas (e.g., lights, joy)
    │   ├── Thanksgiving (e.g., gratitude, table)
    │   ├── Hanukkah (e.g., candles, hope)
    │   └── Kwanzaa (e.g., unity, pride)
    ├── 😊 Moods
    │   ├── Joyful (e.g., festive cheer)
    │   ├── Grateful (e.g., thankful heart)
    │   ├── Hopeful (e.g., new beginnings)
    │   └── Proud (e.g., cultural roots)
    ├── ⭐ Imagery
    │   ├── Lights (e.g., twinkling, candles)
    │   ├── Nature (e.g., snow, harvest)
    │   ├── Objects (e.g., ornaments, food)
    │   └── Moments (e.g., family, community)
    └── ✍ Writing Goals
        ├── Capture a mood
        ├── Use vivid imagery
        ├── Tell a holiday story
        └── Express a feeling
```

Example Poem Using Mind Map (Holiday: Christmas, Mood: Joyful, Imagery: Lights, Goal: Capture a mood):

Christmas lights twinkle, my heart's alight,
Joy sparks bright in the winter night.
My pen holds this festive glow so true.

(By Emma, 15, from California)

Use this mind map on page to plan your poem. Pick one idea from each branch and write for 5–10 minutes. Homeschoolers, this is a dope tool for descriptive writing.

ACTIVITY ZONE

ACTIVITY 1 – ANALYZING CHRISTMAS POEMS

Read this poem by Jaden, 15, from Colorado:

The winter night glows with snowy dreams,
Christmas lights twinkle in starry streams.
My words catch this holiday's joyful spark.

1) What holiday is Jaden's poem about?
a) Thanksgiving
b) Christmas
c) Hanukkah
d) Kwanzaa

2) What imagery from the Holiday Prompt Planner is used?
a) Warm table
b) Twinkling lights
c) Candle glow
d) Unity cup

3) True or False: Jaden's poem uses snowy imagery.

4) Which prompt from the Holiday Glow table did Jaden likely use?
a) "The winter night glows..."
b) "This tradition feels like..."
c) "I'm thankful for this..."
d) "This holiday memory..."

5) Which line shows the holiday mood?
a) The winter night glows with snowy dreams
b) Christmas lights twinkle in starry streams
c) My words catch this holiday's joyful spark
d) All of the above

89

🎯 ACTIVITY ZONE

ACTIVITY 2 – IDENTIFYING GRATITUDE POEMS

Read this poem by Aaliyah, 14, from Georgia:

I'm thankful for this table's love,
Family laughter rising above.
My pen holds this Thanksgiving glow.

1) What holiday is Aaliyah's poem about?
a) Christmas
b) Thanksgiving
c) Hanukkah
d) Winter Solstice

2) What focus from the Thanksgiving and Gratitude table is used?
a) Friends
b) Family
c) Personal Growth
d) Community

3) True or False: Aaliyah's poem mentions family laughter.

4) Which prompt from the Holiday Glow table did Aaliyah likely use?
a) "The winter night glows…"
b) "This tradition feels like…"
c) "I'm thankful for this…"
d) "My holiday wish is…"

5) Which line highlights gratitude?
a) I'm thankful for this table's love
b) Family laughter rising above
c) My pen holds this Thanksgiving glow
d) All of the above

🎯 ACTIVITY ZONE

ACTIVITY 3 – SPOTTING WINTER HOLIDAY VIBES

Read this poem by Noah, 17, from New York:
This tradition feels like a warm hug,
The candle glows on our Hanukkah rug.
My words hold this light, soft and true.

1) What holiday is Noah's poem about?
a) Christmas
b) Thanksgiving
c) Hanukkah
d) Kwanzaa

2) What imagery from the Holiday Prompt Planner is used?
a) Twinkling lights
b) Warm table
c) Candle glow
d) Unity cup

3) True or False: Noah's poem uses a hug metaphor.

4) Which prompt from the Holiday Glow table did Noah likely use?
a) "The winter night glows..."
b) "This tradition feels like..."
c) "I'm thankful for this..."
d) "This holiday memory..."

5) Which line shows the holiday vibe?
a) This tradition feels like a warm hug
b) Candle glow on our Hanukkah rug
c) My words hold this light, soft and true
d) All of the above

ACTIVITY ZONE
ACTIVITY 4 – SPOTTING WINTER HOLIDAY VIBES

Read this poem by Malik, 16, from Florida:
This holiday memory sparkles bright,
Kwanzaa's unity in candlelight.
My words weave our pride, strong and true.

1) What holiday is Malik's poem about?
a) Christmas
b) Thanksgiving
c) Hanukkah
d) Kwanzaa

2) What vibe from the Holiday Prompt Planner is used?
a) Joyful
b) Grateful
c) Hopeful
d) Proud

3) **True or False:** Malik's poem uses candlelight imagery.

4) Which prompt from the Holiday Glow table did Malik likely use?
a) "The winter night glows..."
b) "This tradition feels like..."
c) "This holiday memory..."
d) "My holiday wish is..."

5) Which line shows the holiday memory?
a) This holiday memory sparkles bright
b) Kwanzaa's unity in candlelight
c) My words weave our pride, strong and true
d) All of the above

ANSWERS
ACTIVITY ZONE

ACTIVITY 1 – ANALYZING CHRISTMAS POEMS
1. b) Christmas
2. b) Twinkling lights
3. True
4. a) "The winter night glows…"
5. d) All of the above

ACTIVITY 2 – IDENTIFYING GRATITUDE POEMS
1. b) Thanksgiving
2. b) Family
3. True
4. c) "I'm thankful for this…"
5. d) All of the above

ACTIVITY 3 – SPOTTING WINTER HOLIDAY VIBES
1. c) Hanukkah
2. c) Candle glow
3. True
4. b) "This tradition feels like…"
5. d) All of the above

ACTIVITY 4 – ANALYZING HOLIDAY MEMORIES
1. d) Kwanzaa
2. d) Proud
3. True
4. c) "This holiday memory…"
5. d) All of the above

We'd Love Your Feedback!

Please let us know how we're doing by leaving us a review.

Chapter 8. Craft, Share, and Collect Your Poetry

CHAPTER 8– Craft, Share, and Collect Your Poetry

Learning Objectives

You'll write poems in cool styles (like haiku and spoken word), share them confidently on Instagram or at slams, and curate them into a personal collection that tells your story.

Hey, superstar teen poet! You've poured your heart into poems—now it's time to level up by crafting them in dope styles, sharing them like a pro, and collecting them into a legacy that screams you. This final chapter combines writing in forms like haiku and spoken word, posting with #TeenPoetry, and building a poetry collection that's your vibe. With tables, prompts, a checklist, a flowchart, and activities, you'll shine bright. Snap a pic of your poem with a cool prop (like your journal) and share with #TeenPoetry to join other teen poets. Let's craft, share, and collect your masterpiece!

Why Crafting, Sharing, and Collecting Poetry Is Your Superpower

Your poems are your voice, your truth, your art—and this chapter is your guide to making them pop, sharing them boldly, and curating them into a collection that lasts. Writing in styles like haiku or spoken word (think Amanda Gorman's "fire verses") allows you to play with words. Sharing on Instagram or at a slam builds confidence, while collecting your poems creates a legacy, like a playlist of your life. This triple threat—crafting, sharing, collecting—boosts self-expression and emotional clarity, aligning with SEL goals (per CASEL) and Common Core narrative writing standards. It's also great for essays or SAT/ACT prep. Teachers, use this for creative writing or public speaking units. Parents and homeschoolers, it's the ultimate gift to spark teen creativity. Post with #TeenPoetry or make a Canva reel to join the vibe!

📚 **Teacher Tip:** Use this chapter for poetry slams, digital literacy, or portfolio projects.

Table: Why Crafting, Sharing, and Collecting Slays

Benefit	How It Helps	Example
Creativity	Explores new styles	Writing a haiku about your mood
Confidence	Builds sharing courage	Posting with #TeenPoetry
Legacy	Creates your story	Curating a poetry collection
Connection	Links with others	Performing at a school slam

Example: Here's a haiku by Mia, 16, from California, shared on Instagram:

Stars light up my dreams,
Words dance on my page so free,
My heart's voice takes wing.

Mia said, "This haiku felt like my soul on paper." Ready to craft, share, and collect? Let's dive in!

Poetry Styles That Pop

Poetry styles like haiku, free verse, and spoken word let you play with words and match your vibe. Haiku is short and nature-inspired (5-7-5 syllables), free verse flows without rules, and spoken word is bold and rhythmic. Try them to find your style!

✏️ **How to Use This Table:** Pick a style to write a poem that fits your personality.

🛠️ **Quick Craft Tip**: Match the style to your mood (e.g., haiku for calm, spoken word for energy). Struggling? Try RhymeZone.com for ideas.

✏️ **Table: Poetry Style Cheat Sheet**

Form	Rules	Best For	Example
Haiku	5-7-5 syllables, nature focus	Quiet moments	Moonlight on my page…
Free Verse	No rules, flowing lines	Deep emotions	My heart's a river…
Acrostic	Spell a word with first letters	Personal expression	**B**old words spark my soul…
Spoken Word	Rhythmic, bold, performative	Bold statements	I rise, I roar…

🛠️ **Quick Craft Tip**: Practice your poem aloud for rhythm. Struggling? Try: "My poem's worth sharing because…"

Scaffolded Example (Instagram Post):

- Step: Post on Instagram
- Brainstorm: Bold visuals, short poem
- Draft: My poem's worth sharing because it's me…
- Polished Free Verse (by Jayden, 16, from Texas):

My poem's worth sharing, it's my soul's spark,
A light that glows in the digital dark.
My voice flies free on this screen's bright stage.

Try it: Pick a step from the table, use the action, and write a 4-line poem about sharing. Homeschoolers, this builds digital literacy and confidence.

Building Your Poetry Legacy

Your poems are pieces of you—curate them into a collection that tells your story! Select your best work, choose a theme (e.g., growth, dreams), and sequence them like a playlist for impact. Use the flowchart below to create a legacy you're proud of.

📚 **How to Use This Flowchart**: Follow the steps to build your poetry collection.

📚 **Collection Builder Flowchart**

Start
↓
Select Poems (Choose 5–10 favorites)
↓
Choose Theme (e.g., growth, love)
↓
Order for Impact (Start strong, end memorable)
↓
Add Title (e.g., "My Heart's Playlist")
↓
Finish (Share or keep private)

🛠 **Quick Craft Tip:** Pick a theme that ties your poems together. Struggling?

Try: "My collection is about…"

Scaffolded Example (Theme: Growth):

- Step: Choose Theme
- Brainstorm: Growth, challenges, strength
- Draft: My collection is about rising up…
- Polished Acrostic (by Sofia, 14, from Florida):

Growth blooms in my heart's quiet fight,
Resilient words shine in the light,
Over obstacles, my pen takes flight.

Try it: Use the flowchart on page [insert page number] to plan a 3-poem collection. Write a 4-line poem about your theme. Teachers, this supports portfolio-building.

Prompt Practice: Style, Share, Collect

Time to craft poems in different styles, share them boldly, and add them to your collection! Below are five prompts, each with an example poem in a unique style (haiku, free verse, acrostic, spoken word, blackout poem), a practice prompt to try the style, and tips for sharing and collecting. Write for 5–10 minutes, then use the checklist or flowchart to share or curate. Reflect: How did this style make your voice shine? Would you share or collect it?

✍ **How to Use This Table:** Pick a prompt, read the example, write in the same style, and follow the sharing/collection tip.

Table: 5 Style, Share, Collect Prompts

Style	Example Poem	Practice Prompt	Practice Prompt
Haiku	Moonlight on my dreams,Words whisper hope in the night,My heart finds its peace. (By Aaliyah, 16, from Illinois)	Write a haiku about your favorite place.	**Share:** Post as an Instagram story with #TeenPoetry.**Collect:** Add to a "Calm Vibes" collection.
Free Verse	My soul's a river, wild and free,Flowing through my words for all to see.I'm bold, I'm me, my voice is true. (By Zara, 15, from California)	Write a free verse about your strength.	**Share:** Create a Canva post with bold colors.**Collect:** Start a "Bold Me" collection.
Acrostic	Loud words spark my soul,Inspire the world with my goal,Alive in my truth's glow. (By Liam, 14, from Texas)	Write an acrostic using your name.	**Share:** Post with #YoungPoets.**Collect:** Add to a "My Identity" collection.
Spoken Word	I rise, I roar, my words take flight,Truth's a flame in my starlit night.I'm here, my voice ignites the fight. (By Malik, 17, from Florida)	Write a spoken word poem about your passion.	**Share:** Record a reel for Instagram.**Collect:** End a "Passion" collection with it.
Blackout Poem	Hope shines, fears fade,My voice breaks through the dark. (By Emma, 16, from New York, from a book page)	Create a blackout poem from a magazine about joy.	**Share:** Post a pic of your blackout art.**Collect:** Add to a "Hope" collection.

🎧 Poetry Playlist – Bold Vibes

- "Unstoppable" by Sia
- "Brave" by Sara Bareilles
- "Roar" by Katy Perry

How to Use: Pick a prompt from the table on page [insert page number], write in the given style, and follow the sharing/collection tip. Stuck? Use the Poetry Style Cheat Sheet or RhymeZone.com. ⚡ Challenge Yourself: Combine two styles (e.g., haiku + acrostic) or title your collection (e.g., "My Heart's Playlist"). Teachers, these prompts are great for slam or portfolio submissions. Parents, they're perfect for boosting confidence. Reflect: How did this style amplify your voice?

Example Exercise (Prompt 2, Free Verse):

- Read the Example: Zara's free verse about strength.

- Write Your Poem: Use the practice prompt to write your own free verse.

Exercise: Answer these questions in your journal:

1) What strength did you write about?
a) Emotional
b) Physical
c) Creative
d) Other

2) True or False: Your poem uses a metaphor.

3) Which line feels most shareable?
a) First line
b) Middle line
c) Last line
d) All of them

100

Visual Tool: Poetry Creation Mind Map

[Insert visual diagram of a 4-branch mind map: Styles, Sharing, Collection, Goals]

This mind map helps you craft, share, and collect poems. Start with "Your Poetry" in the center, then branch out to spark ideas.

```
[Your Poetry]
    ├── ✍ Styles
    │    ├── Haiku (e.g., short, nature-based)
    │    ├── Free Verse (e.g., flowing, open)
    │    ├── Acrostic (e.g., name-based)
    │    └── Spoken Word (e.g., bold, rhythmic)
    ├── 📱 Sharing
    │    ├── Instagram (e.g., reels, posts)
    │    ├── Spoken Word (e.g., slams, videos)
    │    └── Friends (e.g., private sharing)
    ├── 📚 Collection
    │    ├── Select Poems (e.g., 5–10 favorites)
    │    ├── Theme (e.g., growth, love)
    │    └── Title (e.g., "My Heart's Playlist")
    └── 😎 Goals
         ├── Express a mood
         ├── Share with pride
         └── Build a legacy
```

Your Turn: Reflective Journal Page

Craft, share, and collect your poetry! Write a poem in one style from 8.4, use the checklist to share it, and add it to your collection. Struggling? Try a fill-in-the-blank: "My voice is __." Check the box when done!

Prompt Checkboxes

☐ Write a haiku about your favorite place.
☐ Create an acrostic using your name.
☐ Record a spoken word reel about your passion and post with #TeenPoetry.

Step	Action	My Plan
✍ Write a Poem	Choose a style	_____
🗒 Add to Collection	Pick a theme	_____
📤 Share It	Use hashtags or perform	_____

Peer Review Quick Guide

Share your poem with a friend or classmate! Use this checklist to give feedback. Example: "Your haiku's peace vibe is strong because 'moonlight' feels so calm!"

⊘ Does the poem match its style (e.g., haiku, spoken word)?
⊘ Can I feel the poet's voice or theme?
⊘ Do the words create a vivid image or mood?
⊘ Is it ready to share or add to a collection?

Mini-Rubric for Teachers

Assess student poems using this rubric:

Style (4 pts): Does the poem follow the chosen form?
Voice (4 pts): Does it sound personal and authentic?
Imagery (4 pts): Are there vivid details or metaphors?
Shareability (4 pts): Is it ready for Instagram, a slam, or a collection?

📜 **Teacher Tip:** Use it for a poetry slam, digital media project, or portfolio assignment.

🎯 ACTIVITY ZONE

ACTIVITY 1 – ANALYZING HAIKU

Read this poem by Aaliyah, 16, from Illinois:

Moonlight on my dreams,
Words whisper hope in the night,
My heart finds its peace.

1) What style is Aaliyah's poem?
a) Free Verse
b) Haiku
c) Acrostic
d) Spoken Word

2) What mood is expressed?
a) Bold
b) Peaceful
c) Passionate
d) Grateful

3) True or False: Aaliyah's poem has a 5-7-5 syllable structure.

4) Which prompt from the Style, Share, Collect table did Aaliyah likely use?
a) Write a haiku about your favorite place
b) Write a free verse about your strength
c) Write an acrostic using your name
d) Write a spoken word poem about your passion

5) Which line creates a calm vibe?
a) Moonlight on my dreams
b) Words whisper hope in the night
c) My heart finds its peace
d) All of the above

🎯 ACTIVITY ZONE

ACTIVITY 2 - IDENTIFYING FREE VERSE

Read this poem by Zara, 15, from California:

My soul's a river, wild and free,
Flowing through my words for all to see.
I'm bold, I'm me, my voice is true.

1) What style is Zara's poem?
a) Haiku
b) Free Verse
c) Blackout Poem
d) Spoken Word

2) What theme is expressed?
a) Peace
b) Strength
c) Gratitude
d) Dreams

3) True or False: Zara's poem uses a river metaphor.

4) Which prompt from the Style, Share, Collect table did Zara likely use?
a) Write a haiku about your favorite place
b) Write a free verse about your strength
c) Write an acrostic using your name
d) Create a blackout poem from a magazine

5) Which line feels most shareable?
a) My soul's a river, wild and free
b) Flowing through my words for all to see
c) I'm bold, I'm me, my voice is true
d) All of the above

🎯 ACTIVITY ZONE
ACTIVITY 3 - SPOTTING ACROSTIC POEMS

Read this poem by Liam, 14, from Texas:

Loud words spark my soul,
Inspire the world with my goal,
A life in my truth's glow.

1) What style is Liam's poem?
a) Haiku
b) Free Verse
c) Acrostic
d) Spoken Word

2) What word is spelled out in the acrostic?
a) LIAM
b) SPARK
c) TRUTH
d) GOAL

3) True or False: Liam's poem uses the word "soul."

4) Which prompt from the Style, Share, Collect table did Liam likely use?
a) Write a haiku about your favorite place
b) Write a free verse about your strength
c) Write an acrostic using your name
d) Write a spoken word poem about your passion

5) Which line shows personal expression?
a) Loud words spark my soul
b) Inspire the world with my goal
c) A live in my truth's glow
d) All of the above

🎯 ACTIVITY ZONE
ACTIVITY 4 – ANALYZING SPOKEN WORD

Read this poem by Malik, 17, from Florida:

I rise, I roar, my words take flight,
Truth's a flame in my starlit night.
I'm here, my voice ignites the fight.

1) What style is Malik's poem?
a) Free Verse
b) Haiku
c) Acrostic
d) Spoken Word

2) What theme is expressed?
a) Peace
b) Passion
c) Gratitude
d) Dreams

3) True or False: Malik's poem uses fire imagery.

4) Which prompt from the Style, Share, Collect table did Malik likely use?
a) Write a haiku about your favorite place
b) Write a free verse about your strength
c) Create a blackout poem from a magazine
d) Write a spoken word poem about your passion

5) Which line feels boldest for sharing?
a) I rise, I roar, my words take flight
b) Truth's a flame in my starlit night
c) I'm here, my voice ignites the fight
d) All of the above

ANSWERS
ACTIVITY ZONE

ACTIVITY 1 – ANALYZING HAIKU

1. b) Haiku
2. b) Peaceful
3. True
4. a) Write a haiku about your favorite place
5. d) All of the above

ACTIVITY 2 – IDENTIFYING FREE VERSE

1. b) Free Verse
2. b) Strength
3. True
4. b) Write a free verse about your strength
5. d) All of the above

ACTIVITY 3 – SPOTTING ACROSTIC POEM

1. c) Acrostic
2. a) LIAM
3. True
4. c) Write an acrostic using your name
5. d) All of the above

ACTIVITY 4 – ANALYZING SPOKEN WORD

1. d) Spoken Word
2. b) Passion
3. True
4. d) Write a spoken word poem about your passion
5. d) All of the above
6. Editable Answer Key: Te

We'd Love Your Feedback!

★ ★ ★ ★ ★

Please let us know how we're doing by leaving us a review.

Chapter 9: Poetry Legacy Lab: Your Story in Verse

CHAPTER 9 – Poetry Legacy Lab: Your Story in Verse

✨ By the End of This Chapter

You'll write 10 poems in 10 unique styles, from free verse to concrete poems, each telling part of your story, using prompts inspired by everything you've learned. Share with #TeenPoetry or build your legacy collection!

Hey, legendary teen poet! This is your Poetry Legacy Lab, where you'll craft 10 poems in 10 different styles to tell your story—your voice, feelings, identity, and vibes from Chapters 1–8. Each prompt has an example poem, a practice prompt for you to try, and a quick exercise to lock in your skills. Use the mind map to spark ideas, then share your faves with #TeenPoetry or add them to your collection. Snap a pic with your journal and post to join other teen poets. Let's create a poetry legacy that's 100% you!

Prompt Practice: 10 Poem Challenge

Write 10 poems in 10 styles, each with an example poem based on a prompt, a practice prompt for you to try, an exercise to check your vibe, and a tip for sharing or collecting. Write for 5–10 minutes per poem, use the mind map on page [insert page number] for inspiration, and reflect: Which poem tells your story best? Post with #TeenPoetry or save for your collection!

🎧 **Poetry Playlist – Legacy Vibes**
- "This Is Me" by The Greatest Showman Ensemble
- "Rise Up" by Andra Day
- "Brave" by Sara Bareilles

Prompt 1: Free Verse (Inspired by Chapter 1: Voice)

Example Prompt: Write a free verse about your unique voice.
Example Poem (by Zara, 16, from California):

My voice is a spark,
Igniting the page with my truth,
A river of words, wild and free,
I'm me, bold and unapologetic.

Prompt 1: Write a free verse about what makes you stand out.

Exercise: Answer these in your journal:

1) What makes you stand out in your poem?
a) Personality
b) Dreams
c) Style
d) Other

2) **True or False:** Your poem has no set rhyme.

3) Which line feels most like you?
a) First line
b) Middle line
c) Last line
d) All of them

3) Did you use a metaphor (e.g., spark, river)?
a) Yes
b) No

4) Would you share this with #TeenPoetry?
a) Yes
b) Maybe
c) No

Share/Collect Tip: Post as a Canva graphic with bold colors; add to a "My Voice" collection.

Prompt 2: Haiku (Inspired by Chapter 8: Styles)

Example Prompt: Write a haiku about a quiet moment.

Example Poem (by Noah, 15, from New York):

Moonlight on my page,
Dreams whisper at night,
Peace flows through my pen.

Practice Prompt: Write a haiku about a favorite memory.

Exercise: Answer these in your journal:
1) What memory did you write about?
a) Family
b) Friends
c) Place
d) Other

2) **True or False:** Your haiku follows a 5-7-5 syllable structure.

3) Which line creates a calm vibe?
a) First line
b) Second line
c) Third line
d) All of them

4) Did you include nature imagery?
a) Yes
b) No

5) Would you post this as an Instagram story?
a) Yes
b) Maybe
c) No

Share/Collect Tip: Share as an Instagram story with #TeenPoetry; add to a "Memories" collection.

Prompt 3: Acrostic (Inspired by Chapter 8: Styles)

Example Prompt: Write an acrostic using the word "DREAM."
Example Poem (by Liam, 14, from Texas):
Daring hopes take flight,
Reaching stars in the night,
Every wish burns bright,
A spark to guide my fight,
Moments that feel so right.

Practice Prompt: Write an acrostic using your name.

Exercise: Answer these in your journal:

1) What word did your acrostic spell?
a) Your name
b) A feeling
c) A place
d) Other

2) **True or False:** Each line starts with a letter of the word.

3) Which line feels most personal?
a) First line
b) Middle line
c) Last line
d) All of them

4) Did you use vivid imagery (e.g., stars, spark)?
a) Yes
b) No

5) Would you add this to your collection?
   1. a) Yes
   2. b) Maybe
   3. c) No

Share/Collect Tip: Post with #YoungPoets; add to an "Identity" collection.

Prompt 4: Letter Poem (Inspired by Chapter 6: Relationships)

Example Prompt: Write a letter poem to a friend who lifts you up.

Example Poem (by Aaliyah, 16, from Illinois):

Dear friend,
Your smile's a light in my storm,
Like sunshine breaking through clouds,
You make my heart feel warm.

Practice Prompt: Write a letter poem to someone who inspires you.

Exercise: Answer these in your journal:

1) Who did you write to?
a) Friend
b) Family
c) Role model
d) Other

2) **True or False:** Your poem starts with "Dear…"

3) Which line shows your feelings?
a) First line
b) Middle line
c) Last line
d) All of them

4) Did you use a simile (e.g., like sunshine)?
a) Yes
b) No

5) Would you share this with the person?
a) Yes
b) Maybe
c) No

Share/Collect Tip: Share privately with them; add to a "Connections" collection.

Prompt 5: Blackout Poem (Inspired by Chapter 8: Styles)

Example Prompt: Create a blackout poem from a book page about courage.
Example Poem (by Emma, 16, from New York):

Strength rises, fears fade,
My heart shines through the dark.
Practice Prompt: Create a blackout poem from a magazine page about joy.

Exercise: Answer these in your journal:

1) What theme did your poem focus on?
a) Joy
b) Courage
c) Hope
d) Other

2) **True or False:** Your poem uses words from the source text.

3) Which line feels most powerful?
a) First line
b) Last line
c) Both
d) Neither

4) Did you create a visual design with your blackout?
a) Yes
b) No

5) Would you post a pic of this poem?
a) Yes
b) Maybe
c) No

Share/Collect Tip: Post a pic of your blackout art; add to a "Joy" collection.

Prompt 6: Spoken Word (Inspired by Chapter 8: Styles)

Example Prompt: Write a spoken word poem about your strength.

Example Poem (by Malik, 17, from Florida):
I rise, I roar, my words ignite,
A flame of truth in the starlit night,
My strength's a fire, bold and bright.

Practice Prompt: Write a spoken word poem about your passion.

Exercise: Answer these in your journal:

1) What passion did you write about?
a) Art
b) Sports
c) Dreams
d) Other

2) True or False: Your poem has a rhythmic flow.

3) Which line feels boldest?
a) First line
b) Middle line
c) Last line
d) All of them

4) Did you use imagery (e.g., flame, night)?
a) Yes
b) No

5) Would you perform this at a slam?
a) Yes
b) Maybe
c) No

Share/Collect Tip: Record a reel for Instagram; add to a "Passion" collection.

Prompt 7: Sonnet (Inspired by Chapter 8: Styles)

Example Prompt: Write a sonnet (14 lines, ABAB CDCD EFEF GG rhyme) about hope.

Example Poem (by Sofia, 14, from Texas):

Hope shines like stars in the darkest of skies,
It lifts my heart when the shadows descend,
A light that glows where my courage lies,
Its spark will guide me to dreams without end.
Through storms of doubt, it remains ever true,
A beacon bright in the chaos of night,
It paints my path with a radiant hue,
And holds me close in its comforting light.
No fear can dim what hope's fire has lit,
It fuels my soul with a boundless desire,
With every step, I grow stronger with it,
This flame of hope sets my spirit on fire.
So I'll hold tight to this glow in my heart,
Hope's light will lead where my dreams find their start.

Practice Prompt: Write a sonnet about a goal you have.

Exercise: Answer these in your journal:

1) What goal did you write about?
a) Career
b) Personal
c) Academic
d) Other

2) True or False: Your sonnet has 14 lines.

3) Which rhyme scheme did you use?
a) ABAB CDCD EFEF GG
b) AABB CCDD EEFF GG
c) No rhyme
d) Other

3) Did you use imagery (e.g., stars, light)?
a) Yes
b) No

4) Would you add this to your collection?
a) Yes
b) Maybe
c) No

Share/Collect Tip: Post as a Canva graphic; add to a "Goals" collection.

Prompt 8: Villanelle (Inspired by Chapter 8: Styles)

Example Prompt: Write a villanelle (19 lines, 5 tercets + quatrain, repeating lines A1 and A2) about dreams.

Example Poem (by Diego, 15, from California):

My dreams ignite my heart each starry night (A1),
They call me forth to worlds I long to roam,
In sleep, my soul takes flight to boundless light (A2).
Through shadows deep, they spark with pure delight,
A fire that glows where fears cannot call home,
My dreams ignite my heart each starry night (A1).
No chains can hold the visions burning bright,
They lift me high above the doubts I've known,
In sleep, my soul takes flight to boundless light (A2).
Each hope I chase grows stronger in my sight,
A path of stars where passion's seeds are sown,
My dreams ignite my heart each starry night (A1).
They weave a tale of courage, taking flight,
A truth that shines where darkness can't be shown,
In sleep, my soul takes flight to boundless light (A2).
So let me dream where no one else can fight,
My heart's alive with every glowing tone,
My dreams ignite my heart each starry night (A1),
In sleep, my soul takes flight to boundless light (A2).

Practice Prompt: Write a villanelle about the theme of courage.

Exercise: Answer these in your journal:

1) What theme did your villanelle explore?
a) Courage
b) Hope
c) Love
d) Other

2) True or False: Your villanelle repeats two lines.

3) How many stanzas does your poem have?
a) 4
b) 5
c) 6
d) Other

4) Did you use vivid imagery?
a) Yes
b) No

5) Would you share this with #TeenPoetry?
a) Yes
b) Maybe
c) No

Share/Collect Tip: Share as a reel; add to a "Courage" collection.

113

Prompt 9: Ode (Inspired by Chapter 5: Aesthetic)

Example Prompt: Write an ode praising your favorite place.
Example Poem (by Amara, 16, from Georgia):
Oh, ocean, you sing with waves of blue,
Your tides pull my heart to shores so wide,
Each crash a song that feels forever new,
Your salty breeze is where my dreams reside.
With every ripple, you paint my soul's view,
Your endless dance is my heart's truest guide.
Practice Prompt: Write an ode praising your favorite season.

Exercise: Answer these in your journal:

1) What season did you praise?
a) Spring
b) Summer
c) Fall
d) Winter

2) True or False: Your ode celebrates something specific.

3) Which line feels most vivid?
a) First line
b) Middle line
c) Last line
d) All of them

4) Did you use descriptive words (e.g., blue, breeze)?
a) Yes
b) No

5) Would you post this as a Canva graphic?
a) Yes
b) Maybe
c) No

Share/Collect Tip: Post with vibrant colors; add to an "Aesthetic" collection.

Prompt 10: Concrete Poem (Inspired by Chapter 5: Aesthetic)

Example Prompt: Write a concrete poem shaped like a tree about growth.

Example Poem (by Linh, 17, from Chicago):

Growing tall, my roots dig deep
In Earth's embrace, I rise to the sky.

Practice Prompt: Write a concrete poem shaped like a star about dreams.

Exercise: Answer these in your journal:

1) What shape did your poem form?
a) Star
b) Heart
c) Tree
d) Other

2) True or False: Your poem's shape matches its theme.

3) Which line feels most visual?
a) First line
b) Middle line
c) Last line
d) All of them

4) Did you arrange words to create a shape?
a) Yes
b) No

5) Would you share a pic of this poem?
a) Yes
b) Maybe
c) No

Share/Collect Tip: Post a pic of your poem's shape; add to a "Dreams" collection.

Visual Tool: Poetry Legacy Mind Map

This mind map sparks ideas for your 10 poems to tell your story. Start with "Your Poetry Legacy" in the center, then branch out to plan your writing.

```
[Your Poetry Legacy]
    ├── ✍ Styles
    │     ├── Free Verse (flowing, open)
    │     ├── Haiku (5-7-5, nature)
    │     ├── Acrostic (spells a word)
    │     ├── Letter Poem (Dear... format)
    │     ├── Blackout Poem (from text)
    │     ├── Spoken Word (bold, rhythmic)
    │     ├── Sonnet (14 lines, rhyme)
    │     ├── Villanelle (repeating lines)
    │     ├── Ode (praise-focused)
    │     └── Concrete Poem (visual shape)
    ├── ⭐ Themes
    │     ├── Voice (Chapter 1)
    │     ├── Emotions (Chapter 3)
    │     ├── Identity (Chapter 4)
    │     ├── Aesthetics (Chapter 5)
    │     ├── Relationships (Chapter 6)
    │     └── Holidays (Chapter 7)
    ├── 📱 Sharing
    │     ├── Instagram (#TeenPoetry, reels)
    │     ├── Spoken Word (slams, videos)
    │     └── Friends (private sharing)
    └── 📚 Collection
          ├── Select Poems (5–10 favorites)
          ├── Theme (e.g., growth, dreams)
          └── Title (e.g., "My Heart's Story")
```

How to Use: Pick one idea from each branch to plan your poem. Write for 5–10 minutes. 📚 Teacher Tip: Use this for creative writing or portfolio projects. Homeschoolers, it's a dope tool for self-expression.

115

Your Turn: Reflective Journal Page

Craft your 10 poems to tell your story! Check the box when done and reflect: Which poem feels most like you? Share with #TeenPoetry or add to your legacy collection.

Prompt Checkboxes

☐ Free Verse: What makes you stand out
☐ Haiku: A favorite memory
☐ Acrostic: Your name
☐ Letter Poem: Someone who inspires you
☐ Blackout Poem: Joy from a magazine
☐ Spoken Word: Your passion
☐ Sonnet: A goal you have
☐ Villanelle: Courage
☐ Ode: Your favorite season
☐ Concrete Poem: A star about dreams

Your Turn: Plan Your Legacy Collection!

Poem #	Style	Theme	Shared? (Y/N)
1	_____	_____	_____
2	_____	_____	_____
3	_____	_____	_____
4	_____	_____	_____
5	_____	_____	_____
6	_____	_____	_____
7	_____	_____	_____
8	_____	_____	_____
9	_____	_____	_____
10	_____	_____	_____

Conclusion and Bonus Content

Conclusion: Your Poetry Journey and What's Next

Wow, you've crushed it! From finding your voice (Chapter 1) to crafting aesthetic vibes (Chapter 5) and building your legacy (Chapter 9), you've turned blank pages into poetry that's all you. You've tackled emotions (Chapter 3), identity (Chapter 4), relationships (Chapter 6), holidays (Chapter 7), and styles like haiku and spoken word (Chapter 8). Each poem boosted your confidence and self-expression, aligning with SEL goals and Common Core standards. Your words are a mirror of your heart—whether you shared them with #TeenPoetry or kept them private, they're powerful.

What's next? Keep writing! Try a 30-day poetry challenge: one poem a day using prompts from this book. Share on Instagram, perform at a school slam, or gift your collection to someone special. Teachers, use this for creative writing or portfolio projects. Parents and homeschoolers, this journal is the ultimate Q4 gift to spark teen creativity. Reflect: How has poetry changed you? Write a 4-line poem about your journey and post it with #TeenPoetry. Your legacy is just beginning—keep creating, keep shining!

Table: Your Poetry Wins

Win	How You Nailed It	Next Step
Voice	Found your unique vibe	Write a poem about your growth
Confidence	Shared with #TeenPoetry	Post a reel or perform at a slam
Creativity	Tried styles like haiku	Experiment with new forms
Legacy	Built a collection	Title it (e.g., *"My Heart's Story"*)

Example Poem (by Jayden, 15, from Texas):

My pen found its fire,
Words carved my truth in the light,
My story's alive,
This poet's ready to fly.

Your Turn: Write a 4-line poem about your poetry journey. Share it or add it to your collection!

Bonus Content

Instagram Poetry Posting Guide

Want to share your poems like a pro? This guide helps you post on Instagram with confidence, inspired by Chapter 8's sharing tips. Whether it's a haiku or spoken word, make your poems pop with #TeenPoetry and connect with other young poets. Here's how to slay your Insta game!

How to Use This Table: Follow these steps to post your poem. Struggling? Try Canva.com for free templates or RhymeZone.com for word ideas.

Table: Instagram Posting Steps

Step	Action	Example
Pick a Poem	Choose one you love	Select your free verse from Chapter 9
Add Visuals	Create a vibe with colors or pics	Use Canva for a dreamy background
Hashtag It	Use #TeenPoetry, #YoungPoets	Add to your post or story
Post with Pride	Share as a reel, story, or post	Caption: "My heart in words #TeenPoetry"

Example Post (by Aaliyah, 16, from Illinois):

Poem: "Moonlight on my dreams, / Words whisper hope in the night…"

Visual: Blue starry background (Canva).

Caption: "Feeling peaceful with this haiku #TeenPoetry"

Your Turn: Pick a poem from Chapter 9, follow the table, and post with #TeenPoetry. Content Note: If sharing feels heavy, start with a private story or share with a friend. Teachers, use this for digital literacy projects.

Track Your Poems

Your poems are your legacy—track them to see your growth! This table helps you log your poems from Chapters 1–9, noting style, theme, and whether you shared them. Use it to plan your collection or celebrate your wins.

How to Use This Table: Log each poem you've written. Struggling? Start with your fave from Chapter 9. Reflect: Which poem are you proudest of?

Table: Poem Tracker

Poem #	Style	Theme	Shared? (Y/N)	Date Written
1	_____	_____	_____	_____
2	_____	_____	_____	_____
3	_____	_____	_____	_____
4	_____	_____	_____	_____
5	_____	_____	_____	_____
6	_____	_____	_____	_____
7	_____	_____	_____	_____
8	_____	_____	_____	_____
9	_____	_____	_____	_____
10	_____	_____	_____	_____

Example Entry (by Malik, 17, from Florida):

- Style: Spoken Word
- Theme: Passion
- Shared: Yes (#TeenPoetry reel)
- Date: August 15, 2025

Your Turn: Log 5 poems from this book in the table. Add a star next to your fave! Homeschoolers, this is great for tracking creative progress. Parents, it's a fun way to see your teen's growth.

Printables Inside

Your journal comes with printable tools to keep your poetry vibe alive! These resources, inspired by Chapters 1–9, include mind maps, tables, and journal pages to spark creativity. Download them from [insert website link] or scan the QR code in the book.

How to Use This Table: Check out these printables to boost your writing. Struggling? Start with the Voice Finder Mind Map from Chapter 1.

Table: Printable Tools Overview

Printable	Inspired by Chapter	Use It For	Example
Voice Finder Mind Map	1 (Voice)	Finding your vibe	Brainstorm emotions, dreams
Emotion Wheel	3 (Emotions)	Pinpointing feels	Write about joy, loneliness
Identity Map	4 (Identity)	Exploring you	Map family, hobbies
Aesthetic Mood Board	5 (Aesthetic)	Crafting vibes	Pick colors, textures
Poem Tracker	10 (Bonus)	Logging poems	Track style, theme

Example Use (by Emma, 16, from New York):

Printable: Aesthetic Mood Board
Use: Planned a concrete poem with a "dreamy" mood, blue colors.
Result: "My star-shaped poem felt so me!"

Your Turn: Pick one printable from the table, download it, and use it to write a poem. Share with #TeenPoetry or add to your collection. Teachers, use these for classroom writing stations.

Your Turn: Reflective Journal Page

Reflect on your poetry journey and keep creating! Write a 4-line poem about how poetry has changed you, then plan your next steps with the checklist below.

Your Poem: Below is just a sample , you write your own.

Poetry cracked my heart wide open,
set it free, Words became my shield,
my truth, my spree.
From silent doubts to verses bold and true,
I found my voice, and now I'm breaking through.

Next Steps Checklist for Your Poetry Journey
- Write one new poem this week, experimenting with a new form (e.g., haiku, sonnet, or free verse).
- Read a poem by a contemporary American poet (e.g., Amanda Gorman or Ocean Vuong) for inspiration.
- Could you share a poem with a friend, teacher, or online community for feedback?
- Join a local or online poetry club or workshop to connect with other teen poets.
- Keep a small notebook or use a phone app to jot down daily ideas or lines that spark creativity.

Poetry Next Steps Checklist

☐ Write a poem a day for 30 days using prompts from Chapters 1–9.
☐ Share a poem with #TeenPoetry or at a school slam.
☐ Complete your Poem Tracker (Bonus Content).
☐ Download a printable from [insert website link].
☐ Title your collection (e.g., "My Heart's Story").

How to Use: Write your poem, check off at least two steps, and reflect: How will you keep your poetry vibe going? Post your poem with #TeenPoetry or save it for your collection. Parents, this is a fun way to encourage creativity!

🎧 Final Playlist – Keep the Vibe Going
- "Roar" by Katy Perry
- "Unstoppable" by Sia
- "This Is Me" by The Greatest Showman Ensemble

Appendix

APPENDIX -A : POETRY POWER WORDS

Hey, teen poet! Want your poems to pop? This Poetry Power Words table gives you 5 vivid words to make your writing bold and expressive. Use them to spark emotions or images!

✏️ **How to Use**: Pick a word and write a 4-line poem with it. Need inspo? Think about how the word feels to you.

Word	Meaning	Example Line
Radiant	Bright, glowing	My heart's radiant with hope
Whisper	Soft, quiet sound	Dreams whisper in the night
Ignite	Spark or set on fire	My words ignite the page
Shimmer	Soft, sparkling light	Stars shimmer in my soul
Surge	Powerful rush	A surge of joy lifts me

Example Poem (by Aaliyah, 16, from Illinois):

My dreams whisper soft and low,
Guiding me where stars will glow,
A spark to light my heart's true show,
I write, and my soul starts to grow.

Your Turn: Pick a word from the table, write a 4-line poem, and share it with #TeenPoetry or keep it in your journal.

APPENDIX -B : POETRY STARTERS

Stuck starting a poem? This Poetry Starters table gives you 5 opening lines to kick off your writing. Each sets a vibe to get your pen moving fast!

✏️ **How to Use:** Choose a starter and finish the poem with 3–5 more lines. Make it about your life or feelings.

Starter Line	Vibe	Try This
My heart is a…	Emotional	Compare to something bold
Under the stars…	Dreamy	Describe a night moment
I rise like…	Powerful	Use a strong image
In my world…	Personal	Share your unique view
The wind carries…	Poetic	Write about a feeling

Example Poem (by Noah, 15, from New York):

Under the stars I find my peace,
Moonlight paints my dreams in blue,
Each wish a spark that won't cease,
My heart's alive, my words are true.

Your Turn: Pick a starter, write a short poem, and add it to your journal or post with #TeenPoetry.

APPENDIX - C : HOW TO APPROACH POETRY

Not sure how to start writing? This How to Approach Poetry table gives you 5 ways to dive into poetry with confidence. Each approach helps you find your flow!

✎ **How to Use:** Pick an approach, follow the steps, and write a quick poem. Try a new one each time you write.

Approach	Steps	Example
Freewrite	Write without stopping for 2 min	Jot down random thoughts
Image First	Picture a scene, then describe	Waves crash on a shore
Emotion Dump	Name a feeling, write about it	"I'm angry, like a storm…"
Word Play	Pick 3 words, weave them in	Use "hope," "fire," "sky"
Memory Lane	Recall a moment, write it	Your best friend's laugh

Example Poem (by Malik, 17, from Florida, Emotion Dump):

I'm angry, like a storm's fierce roar,
My words crash loud, they break the door,
Yet in my pen, I find my core,
Peace grows where rage was before.

Your Turn: Choose an approach, write a poem, and share it with a friend or #TeenPoetry.

APPENDIX - D : COMMON GRAMMAR FIXES FOR POETRY

Mistakes happen, but your poems can still shine! This Common Grammar Fixes for Poetry table lists 5 frequent errors with quick fixes to keep your words clear.

✎ **How to Use:** Check your poem for these errors and fix them. Write a new poem to practice clean grammar.

Error	Fix	Example
Run-on Sentence	Add periods or commas	"I run I fly" → "I run. I fly."
Wrong Their/There	Use "their" for people, "there" for place	"There hearts" → "Their hearts"
No Punctuation	Add commas or dashes for flow	"I dream I soar" → "I dream, I soar"
Misspelled Words	Double-check words	"Shinning" → "Shining"
Overused "And"	Replace with stronger words	"And I feel" → "Then I feel"

Example Poem (by Sofia, 14, from Texas, Fixed Run-on):

My heart beats fast. It soars with light,
Each word I write feels strong, feels right,
No chains can hold my dreams tonight,
I rise, I shine, I take my flight.

Your Turn: Write a 4-line poem, check for these errors, and fix them. Keep it in your journal or share with #TeenPoetry.

YOUNG WRITER SERIES - DR. FANATOMY

Please let us know how we're doing by leaving us a review.

www.ingramcontent.com/pod-product-compliance
Lightning Source LLC
Chambersburg PA
CBHW081401070526
44583CB00020B/2621